MERE CATHOLICISM

To Anne and George Holmes

MERE CATHOLICISM

IAN KER

EMMAUS
ROAD
PUBLISHING
Steubenville, Ohio
A Division of Catholics United for the Faith

Emmaus Road Publishing
827 North Fourth Street
Steubenville, OH 43952

Library of Congress Control Number: 2006910319
ISBN: 1-931018-39-1

Unless otherwise indicated, Scripture quotations are taken
from the Revised Standard Version, Catholic Edition (RSVCE)
© 1965, 1966 by the Division of Christian Education of the
National Council of the Churches of Christ in the
United States of America. Used by permission.

Cover design and layout by
Beth Hart

CONTENTS

Contents

ABBREVIATIONS

The Old Testament
Gen./Genesis
Ex./Exodus
Lev./Leviticus
Num./Numbers
Deut./Deuteronomy
Josh./Joshua
Judg./Judges
Ruth/Ruth
1 Sam./1 Samuel
2 Sam./2 Samuel
1 Kings/1 Kings
2 Kings/2 Kings
1 Chron./1 Chronicles
2 Chron./2 Chronicles
Ezra/Ezra
Neh./Nehemiah
Tob./Tobit
Jud./Judith
Esther/Esther
Job/Job
Ps./Psalms
Prov./Proverbs
Eccles./Ecclesiastes
Song/Song of Solomon

Wis./Wisdom
Sir./Sirach (Ecclesiasticus)
Is./Isaiah
Jer./Jeremiah
Lam./Lamentations
Bar./Baruch
Ezek./Ezekiel
Dan./Daniel
Hos./Hosea
Joel/Joel
Amos/Amos
Obad./Obadiah
Jon./Jonah
Mic./Micah
Nahum/Nahum
Hab./Habakkuk
Zeph./Zephaniah
Hag./Haggai
Zech./Zechariah
Mal./Malachi
1 Mac./1 Maccabees
2 Mac./2 Maccabees

The New Testament
Mt./Matthew
Mk./Mark
Lk./Luke
Jn./John
Acts/Acts of the Apostles
Rom./Romans
1 Cor./1 Corinthians
2 Cor./2 Corinthians
Gal./Galatians
Eph./Ephesians
Phil./Philippians
Col./Colossians
1 Thess./1 Thessalonians
2 Thess./2 Thessalonians
1 Tim./1 Timothy
2 Tim./2 Timothy
Tit./Titus
Philem./Philemon
Heb./Hebrews
Jas./James
1 Pet./1 Peter
2 Pet./2 Peter
1 Jn./1 John
2 Jn./2 John
3 Jn./3 John
Jude/Jude
Rev./Revelation (Apocalypse)

FOREWORD
Walter Hooper

The title *Mere Catholicism* is, of course, meant to remind us of C. S. Lewis's classic *Mere Christianity* (1952). While there are important differences between them, I am an admirer of both. Whereas Lewis's book was originally given as radio talks addressed to believers and unbelievers alike, Father Ian Ker is writing not only for Christians and non-Christians but to confirm Catholics in their beliefs.

C. S. Lewis's *Mere Christianity* consists of four series of talks given over the BBC between 1941 and 1944, and published as a book in 1952. Each talk was only about ten minutes long. Lewis, however, had an uncanny ability to express profound truth in everyday language, and that is why his book is read and re-read. Because Protestant beliefs differ in various ways, Lewis limited his talks to those things nearly all Christians have in common—what he called "mere" Christianity. Much of the usefulness of that book depends on it being limited. "Some people," Lewis said in the Preface to *Mere Christianity*, "draw unwarranted conclusion from the fact that I never say more about the Blessed Virgin Mary. . . . But surely my reason for not doing so is obvious? To say more would take me at once into highly controversial regions. . . . One of the things Christians are disagreed about is the importance of their disagreements."

It may surprise some Catholics to know that *Mere Christianity* has played a large part in many conversions to Catholicism. I have seen *Mere Christianity* referred to in the United States as "a great Catholic classic," and, of course, it is Catholic in the sense that all the great doctrines Lewis illuminates—the Incarnation, the Atonement, the Resurrection—are

Catholic doctrines. So while "mere Christianity" is by no means all there is, it is very clear about the essentials that it addresses.

I converted from Anglicanism to the Catholic Church in 1988 mainly because, quite simply, I believed the claims of the Catholic Church to be true. What led me to believe those claims were— besides *Mere Christianity*—such unashamedly Catholic books as Cardinal Newman's *Apologia Pro Vita Sua* (1864), and *An Essay on the Development of Christian Doctrine* (1845). I was particularly affected by the suggestion in Cardinal Newman's *Development of Christian Doctrine* (II, iii, 5) that if Saint Athanasius or Saint Ambrose came suddenly to life "it cannot be doubted what communion he would take to be his own." And were those saints to travel northwards to Oxford, "the holy brothers would turn from many a high aisle and solemn cloister which they found there, and ask the way to some small chapel where mass was said in the populous alley or forlorn suburb." I was more than happy to give up Anglican high aisles and solemn cloisters for the small chapel where Mass was said.

However, having exchanged the "high aisles and solemn cloisters" for the Catholic chapel, where were the *modern* books on Catholicism? Was there a *Catholic* "mere Christianity"? More to the point, where was "mere Catholicism"? It was a matter of regret that I did not respond to the claims of the Catholic Church sooner, and I think I would have responded sooner if I had come across a book that stated simply and solely what one might call "The *case* for Catholicism."

Then on the evening of May 26, 1992, I went to a meeting of the Oxford University C. S. Lewis Society. Father Ian Ker, the eminent Newman scholar, gave a talk on *Mere Christianity* which he said greatly influenced him in his teens. He was, however, the first speaker at this Society who pointed out that *Mere Christianity*, for all its brilliance, was not enough. As he talked, I realized that my love for Lewis and his books had blinded me to the shortcomings of this wonderful elucidation of the fundamentals of Christianity. Father Ker drew our attention to a statement of Newman which threw the whole thing into a completely new light.

He mentioned an essay by Newman written in 1838, which he quotes in the *Apologia Pro Vita Sua*, in which he made clear why "mere Christianity" was insufficient in itself. Although Newman was still a few years off from his conversion to the Catholic Church, he provides, in one stroke, the main difference between Protestantism and Catholicism. He pointed out that the Church of England believed that there existed something "definite in its outline . . . recognized as the faith," which is the "property of each individual." And because this faith, which certainly sounds like Lewis's "mere Christianity," is the "property of each individual," an individual Christian "may battle for it in his day," even against the Church of England, should that church fail to hold to this clearly defined faith.

Having defined the Protestant view of the fundamentals of the faith, Newman went on to show how it differs from Catholicism. The "peculiarity" of this Protestant doctrine is that

> It supposed the Truth to be entirely objective and detached, not lying hid in the bosom of the Church as if one with her, clinging to her and (as it were) lost in her embrace, but as being sole and unapproachable as on the Cross or at the Resurrection, with the Church close by, but in the background.

Father Ker went on to quote the passage in the *Apologia* in which the difference between Protestantism and Catholicism is shown to be a "contrast presented to us between the Madonna and Child, and a Calvary." To the Protestant those various elements, which make up "mere Christianity," may be viewed as "objective and detached" objects upon a hillside—a "Calvary." The Protestant sees up there on the hill such objective doctrines as the Incarnation, the crucifixion, and the Resurrection. He hopes that his church, "close by but in the background," believes them and holds on to them. There is, unhappily, a good chance that it will not, in which case he will have to hold on to them by himself.

But to the Catholic, said Father Ker, quoting Newman, these great truths are by no means "objective and detached" like a Calvary, but "hid in the bosom of the Church as if one with her, clinging to her and (as it were) lost in her embrace." That is why we call her *Mother Church.* "Mere Christianity" is not something foreign to her, but is indeed her own child, something she is the Mother *of.* The idea of detaching "mere Christianity"—or perhaps I should say simply "Catholic beliefs"—from the Church is inconceivable.

His words struck me like a bolt of lightning, and when I wrote up my diary that evening I said: "I was stunned by the talk, and I know that if I weren't already a Catholic this would have caused me to convert. . . . Father Ker insisted that *Mere Christianity* was a great book, but he held his ground about there being such a thing as "mere Christianity" which can be met outside the Catholic Church."

After that evening I was keener than ever to find a book devoted solely to "mere Catholicism." I wonder if the fact that there did not seem to be one is explained by that other spiritual classic from the pen of C. S. Lewis, *The Screwtape Letters* (1940). That work consists of a series of imaginary letters from a senior tempter from hell, Screwtape, to a junior devil, Wormwood, on the art of temptation. In Letter 25, Screwtape tells the junior tempter, "What we want, if men become Christians at all, is to keep them in the state of mind I call "Christianity And." You know, Christianity and the crisis, Christianity and the new psychology, Christianity and . . .'"

Screwtape is obviously behind the creation of "Catholicism And." If so, perhaps that explains why so many publishers appear to believe that Catholicism should never be taken on its own and is only palatable when mixed with other things. I dare even to suggest that a misunderstanding of what the Catholic Church means by "Church Unity" can be so used. Probably no one was as committed to unity between Christians as the beloved Pope John Paul II, but he never suggested that Catholicism should be *diluted* in the interest of unity. "This unity," we are told in the *Catechism* (820), "subsists in the Catholic Church as something she can never lose, and we hope that it will continue to increase until the end of time. . . . The desire to recover the unity of all Christians is a gift of Christ and a call of the Holy Spirit."

What, then, is the difference between *Mere Christianity* and *Mere Catholicism?* "I hope no reader," said Lewis in the Preface to his book, "will suppose that 'mere' Christianity is here put forward as an alternative to the creeds of the existing communions—as if a man could adopt it in preference to Congregationalism or Greek Orthodoxy or anything else." *Mere Christianity* is not an end in itself, but a pointer to something far greater.

Or, as Father Ker says in the Preface to this book, "'mere Catholicism' is in fact 'mere Christianity' . . . drawn to its logical conclusion." And that conclusion is, as the readers of this book will discover, what Cardinal Newman called "the One true Fold of the Redeemer." This book is surely destined to become a Catholic classic.

—WALTER HOOPER
Literary Advisor to the Estate of C. S. Lewis

PREFACE

It was the seventeenth-century Puritan Richard Baxter who coined the phrase "mere Christianity." By that he meant what C. S. Lewis called "the belief that has been common to nearly all Christians at all times." Lewis borrowed the phrase for his own famous book, in which he sought to explain and justify what are often described as the "fundamentals" of Christianity.

I have adapted the phrase for this book in which I have attempted to set out the fundamentals of Catholicism. Here I have an advantage over Lewis, since the doctrines the Catholic Church believes to be fundamental have been explicitly defined by the Church as doctrines which are essential to Christian faith; whereas there is considerable disagreement among non-Catholic Christians about the fundamentals of "mere Christianity."

I use the word "mere" for another reason altogether, a sense that Lewis certainly didn't have in mind. For by "mere Catholicism" I also mean something like "this is all Catholicism is." Or, to put it another way, "mere Catholicism" is in fact "mere Christianity." It is, if you like, Christianity drawn to its logical conclusion. For example, once you take seriously the fact that the virgin birth only took place because Mary assented to the divine message, then you start to realize that, far from being simply the biological channel used by God, Mary actually played an active role in our redemption by helping to make possible the Incarnation.

I think that many people imagine that Catholicism is Christianity plus a whole lot of other unnecessary or weird (or worse) doctrines and practices added on. My aim in this little book is to show that "mere Christianity" simply implies and leads on to what I call "mere Catholicism." So, although Catholicism *is* complex, because after all it is, I believe, the key to understanding a very complex world; nevertheless, it is entirely simple and straightforward as the unfolding of "mere Christianity."

I am very grateful to the Rev. Dr. Richard Barrett and the Rev. Dr. Philip Egan for scrutinizing the manuscript and for their criticisms and suggestions.

CHAPTER I

THE UNAVOIDABLE QUESTION

"What's it worth?" "Is it worth the trouble?" "Is there any point in it?" "What does this mean?" Our daily lives are filled with questions about the value or worth of people and things and about their meaning and point. We would be very surprised indeed if we met somebody who just couldn't see the purpose or use of such questions. The reason for this is quite simple. Human beings are rational: they naturally seek intelligibility and meaning, they want to know what the point or purpose of something is; they can't help being interested in what something's worth, how much value to place on somebody's word.

Now there is a further question that people cannot help asking: has life itself any meaning or value beyond this world? A philosopher like Bertrand Russell may retort that the question is meaningless, since it makes no sense to talk about meaning or value except in terms of this life and the world we know. But this reaction to a perfectly intelligible question, indeed a question that can be called the question of all questions, which has exercised human minds since the beginning of recorded time, does sound a little too clever by half. Could it be, one can't help suspecting, just a clever way of simply saying "no" to the question? Maybe, but the interesting thing is that the philosopher to whom I am referring didn't just do that. It is as if he recognized that people do in fact ask this ultimate question as if it were a sensible question to ask and one that deserved an answer. So, instead of contenting himself with the answer that this life has no meaning or ultimate value, he preferred to argue that the question is meaningless and, therefore, doesn't deserve a reply because it shouldn't have been posed in the first place. Well, no doubt that's a clever way of pre-empting the question. But clever philosophers aren't necessarily either the most morally serious people or the most sensible of people. For the truth is that people do ask this question as if it were not only perfectly meaningful but also very well worth asking, so much so that it could be said to be the most important of all questions, whether or not an answer can be found to it.

Perhaps the most obvious starting point for most people through the ages is the existence of good and evil. True, clever philosophers have tried hard to explain away good and evil in the sense of explaining them in purely human terms as though they imply or suggest nothing that can't be understood in relation to this life and the world we know. In other words, they don't point to anything or anybody outside this world. However, that is not how it strikes all philosophers. Many philosophers acknowledge that different cultures and societies may vary somewhat in their moral codes, but, in spite of all these variations, there is a universal recognition of the existence of good and evil, of the fact of moral obligation. The mere fact that it is possible for people to criticize the morality in which they were brought up suggests that our sense of good and evil cannot be reduced to the principles and standards of the environment in which we were raised. It makes perfectly good sense to stand back and ask myself if a particular moral belief of mine is right or wrong. And this ability to criticize one's own values adds to the sense that the voice of conscience comes from outside both oneself and society. If so, could it be the echo of the voice of God?

For those who wish to deny that conscience has any such supernatural authority, the real explanation for the authoritative voice of conscience lies not just in the current norms of a particular society but in the universal experience of human beings trying to live together in harmony and peace with one another and in the consequent need to establish moral norms of behavior. Even if this explanation does justice to the sheer force of conscience, it nevertheless still does not account for private personal morality. After all, cruel or malicious thoughts, for example, don't do anyone any harm, unless acted on, and yet we do in fact experience the voice of conscience even in our innermost feelings and thoughts to which no one else has access. Of course, it could be argued that we only have such twinges of conscience because such evil feelings and thoughts can so easily lead to actions that will harm others. But does this explanation really do justice to our sense of personal imperfection, to our awareness of how far our hearts are from being loving? Would we not suffer guilt and remorse if we were marooned on a desert island with no possibility of rescue, no chance of ever being able to affect others with our uncharity, our selfishness, our bad temper, our pride, our greed, our lust?

If conscience suggests a supernatural source for itself, then it also tells us that God is both personal and moral. But there is the other reason for believing in God that we have mentioned and which similarly gives us information about Him, and that is the universal feeling that this life has a significance and value which protest against mortality and which demand fulfillment in a continuing existence. In fact, it is not just a feeling or hope but a reasonable intuition which postulates a Creator who gives us this significance and value and who therefore must Himself embody them while transcending the goodness of human life. For some, then, it will be this sense of meaning and purpose which runs through life that indicates an afterlife where we shall attain our full potential and find that plenitude of happiness which eludes us in this life.

It is perfectly arguable that religious faith does not require justification; it is self-evidently desirable and meaningful in itself. If it carries its own intrinsic value like art or nature, then it seems otiose to try and find a basis for it, since it will be self-justifying. If religious faith can make people good and happy and fulfilled, is there any need for further argument? After all, if we are to be empirical and go on the evidence, then the results of faith will be very pertinent. Likewise, well-authenticated miracles that purport to be the effect of prayer may be another proof of God's existence.

At this point we must say something about this word "proof" in the religious context. When we speak about proofs here, we are certainly not talking about the kind of proofs that we expect in science and logic. Since, if God is God, He is "outside" the world like an author is "outside" his or her book, His existence cannot be proved scientifically as He is not part of the observable world. It is true that we can find evidence for God's existence in the world just as we infer from a book the existence of an author or perhaps authors. In the same way that we infer things about an author from his book, we can learn about God from His world. Again, it is a logical truth—true by definition of the words—that if God is good then He cannot be bad; but there is no way we can logically prove the existence of God any more than we can logically prove that a book has one author rather than several. We simply can't put that kind of truth in the form of a syllogism. But then how many of the truths of which we are convinced can be proved logically or scientifically? I have every reason to suppose I will die one day and I would be a fool to deny the fact; but clearly my future death cannot be scientifically verified until I am dead, nor can I construct any kind of logical syllogism by which to arrive at this patent truth. Or a man's most important conviction in life may be the fact that his wife loves him, but this is not something he can prove to a doubting skeptic. There was no way that Desdemona in Shakespeare's *Othello* could prove logically or scientifically that she was a faithful and loving wife to Othello—but she knew that she was, and so should Othello have known.

That word "should" is worth noting. While we blame Othello for not knowing a fact like that, we don't say he was stupid as we would if a logical or scientific truth was put before his eyes. A question of trust enters into a case like this. So many of the most obvious truths in life, as well as some of the most important ones—or rather the most important ones if we think that the truth about our affections is more important than anything else in life—are just not verifiable by either logical or scientific proof. Yet the odd thing is that people commonly make this grounds for not believing in the existence of God or the truth of Christianity, when every day of their lives they hold, and without any hesitation profess, as certain truths about all kinds of things they can't begin to prove logically or scientifically.

We can, then, have excellent, indeed overwhelming, arguments for God's existence, but let us not confuse ourselves by trying to pretend that they must be like the kind of arguments that we use quite properly to prove that I am sitting at a desk or that, if I am sitting down, then I cannot also be standing up. Knowing about God is much more like knowing that somebody loves me. We would be surprised if somebody demanded logical or scientific proofs for something that we know not through our eyes or our brains but in our heart.

In a similar way we can *know* that God exists in our conscience. This kind of reason for believing in a God derives from the nature of human life. It also tells us something about the nature of God. Other arguments may, for some people, be even more compelling, but they are less informative about the nature of God. For instance, the beauty of art and nature may induce a religious outlook. In that case, the idea that a purely chemical or physical explanation for existence will seem fantastic. But beauty doesn't tell us that God is all-good and all-loving. Nor do other arguments drawn from the physical world. The order that exists in the universe, and particularly the human brain, which is the most complex example of design known to us and through which we discern the world's design, indicates that the world has been designed by a designer. This implies a superhuman intelligence, but, again, tells us nothing about a God of love. The same is true of the argument from causality, which in essence is the argument that everything in the world must have an explanation or reason for existing, which in turn implies that the universe as a whole must have a first or uncaused or transcendent cause. Or, to put it more simply, the universe simply doesn't explain itself.

Now what is important to note is that all these different reasons for believing in God, however much or little they tell us about Him, are *personal* ones—that is to say, in each case, only a personal reality as opposed to an impersonal force makes sense of the evidence. Even so, many people prefer to say, when pressed, that they believe in "something" rather than "someone." One can understand why. Believing in a thing as opposed to a person commits one to less. In particular, believing in "someone out there" would imply that that person might speak to one, make demands on one; whereas "something out there" is less demanding, even less threatening. But by the same token, a person can offer more than a thing. The reality is that in this, as in so many other less important matters in life, people are inconsistent. Their reasons for belief, or at least for hope, in an afterlife and a meaning and purpose to life imply not "something out there" but "Someone out there."

One obvious reason why a thing rather than a Person is easier to imagine and therefore believe in is that in the developed world, unlike the third world, extraordinary economic and technological progress has gone hand in hand with a catastrophic decline in the quality of family and community life. For people who may not have experienced a human father who provided stability in childhood, the idea of a Father who is Creator is likely to be correspondingly harder to envisage. Similarly, the wider breakdown of social relationships does not encourage or foster membership in a religious community. The idea of a spiritual society which enhances personal fulfillment and happiness becomes remote from actual experience and, therefore, less credible.

It is easy, though, to understand why so many people prefer to hedge their bets. Not only is the concept of a divine thing potentially less demanding, but it also requires less belief because it involves less and promises less. But, paradoxically, it is only a belief in "Someone out there" that meets most of the reasons for believing in anything at all. The expectations that are natural to human beings are consistent with a personal God, not with an impersonal entity. A super-athlete is not somebody who is not an athlete at all, but an athlete who is endowed with exceptional abilities. Similarly, the supernatural and the superhuman mean not that which is not natural and not human but that which is more than natural, more than human. A transcendent God is not a God who transcends humanity in the sense of leaving the human behind but in the sense of being more than human. A personal God does not transcend personality in the sense of superseding personality but in the sense of adding a higher dimension to personality. The Jewish revelation, which Christianity claims to transcend, not in the sense of rejecting but in the sense of augmenting by fulfilling, holds that human beings are created in the image of God, which means that they resemble their Creator. But if they are like God in the sense of reflecting His nature, and experience their need for God in terms of the human personality, then this God must be a *personal* God in ways that make sense to a human being with a human personality. This God must not be more than the human person in the absurd sense of being *less* than the human person. This God must be all that a human person is but far more, not in an impersonal but in a personal way. A grown-up is not a different kind of being from a child but rather a child who has grown up.

Now if a personal God is the only kind of a God that is worth believing in—in the sense that an impersonal God does not correspond to the reasons why human beings have always felt a need for believing in some kind of a supernatural reality—then this God must be personal in the ways that human beings are persons, but in an infinite and transcendent way. When we think of how human beings differ even from those animals which seem most like human beings in their instincts, feelings, and intelligence, we are confronted by that phenomenon we call self-consciousness and the capacity to reflect on ourselves. Even the most intelligent and sensitive animals lack this capability. For example, an animal can react acutely to pain, but, so far as we can tell, it does not have a consciousness of the experience of pain in the way that human beings not only feel pain but are aware, for example, of the length and the nature of the pain suffered. The difference is between suffering pain and being aware of suffering pain, an extra factor which, of course, increases the suffering. Or again, highly intelligent animals like dogs can be trained not to act in ways that displease their owners, and even to be aware of the displeasure they cause when they break the rules. Or again, the loyalty of a dog to its owner may seem practically human, but it remains an instinctive rather than a conscious loyalty. We simply cannot speak of even the most intelligent animals as possessing the self-awareness with which human beings are endowed.

A personal God, therefore, must have the qualities that characterize human beings, but to an infinite extent and in a transcendent way. I have hinted above that, while we might try and explain human intelligence, love, and even conscience in terms that would differentiate humans from animals in a quantitative rather than qualitative way, it is this capacity for looking at ourselves, for examining critically our thinking processes, our ability to love others, and our moral principles, that puts us in a unique situation in the world of sentient beings. Now, the curious thing is that when we discuss or evaluate or analyze ourselves, it is as though we are talking about another person. The fact that I can talk or think about me, as though "me" were somebody else, is not only a uniquely human capacity but it also provides a key to understanding the Christian idea of God.

CHAPTER 2

GOD AND US

A personal God who really is a personal God, as opposed to a divine entity or essence, must certainly possess all those characteristics which constitute the human person but to a superhuman extent. However, if self-consciousness is what makes a human being essentially—infinitely, one might say—different from the most high-powered computer or the most affectionate and intelligent of animals, so too a personal God must possess an analogous power of self-awareness and self-reflection.

Our mysterious ability to distance ourselves from ourselves as though our "self" were distinct from our person—that ability to, so to speak, look at ourselves from the outside—must be an endowment of a personal God as well. That is to say, a God who is a personal God must also be able, presumably, to be aware that He is God and also to have, in the appropriate godly way, feelings and thoughts about Himself. God must be able to look at what constitutes God, what is the essence and nature of God.

The Jewish Old Testament speaks of the Wisdom of God as active and present in the world, and this Wisdom becomes the Word of God in the Christian New Testament, taking flesh and humanity in Jesus Christ. The Wisdom or Word of God is God's self-expression. When we look at ourselves we have—or should have—mixed feelings and thoughts. We like some parts of ourselves, but other aspects and elements will arouse negative reactions. This is because we are not perfect beings, but a mixture of good and bad. God is obviously in a very different situation. When God considers

God, He can only fully approve the perfection that is God. As human beings, we are and do many things, but whatever admiration people may have for various human abilities and talents, at the end of the day we all know deep down that there is nothing superior to goodness. And by goodness I don't mean just good actions and deeds. There are people who are full of what are called "good works" who don't elicit our highest admiration. The clue to why this is so is that we don't necessarily love such people; we may even be repelled by them. Whatever people's religion, or lack of religion, it is those human beings who show the most love for others who ultimately are most admired. It is not therefore surprising that Christianity, which considers that human beings are created in the image of God, should also regard God as, above all else, Love itself.

One of the New Testament writers, Saint John, who defines God as Love, begins his Gospel by declaring that the Word pre-existed the creation of the world, and that this Word was not only in or with God but was God. In the Jewish Old Testament the Word of God is understood to mean not only verbal utterances but also the acts and deeds which reveal God. The Christian New Testament, aware that the Old Testament speaks of the Wisdom of God as though a person, makes the Word of God synonymous with and yet somehow distinct from God. How can God the Father, that is, the Creator of all that is, be the same as and yet not the same as his self-expression? The analogy of the human person who can both be detached from self and yet not be someone else offers a clue.

As I said, when we consider our own self we have mixed reactions; but evidently when God does the divine equivalent, God can entertain nothing but absolute love for His own self as that self is His self-expression. When Love expresses itself, it must love its self-expression. Instead of the inevitable human mixture of like and dislike, of love and hatred that we experience when we look at the way we express ourselves, God can only have unmixed love for God, as God expresses Himself as Love. We can look at ourselves in a mirror and if we smile with pleasure at our reflection, the reflection in the mirror will smile back at us. We like what we see and our reflection smiles back with pleasure at its origin, our face. When Love looks at its self-expression, its self-manifestation, its self-revelation, Love can only love what it contemplates; and, when Love's expression looks at its source which is Love, it can only love what it sees. Unlike our smile in the mirror which has no existence in itself, the smile of divine Love does have a dynamic life of its own, although never independently or separately from its source, Love. The analogy therefore breaks down because we are now talking about the infinite, but perhaps it serves a purpose in illustrating how, in human terms, we can love our (self-) expression and how our expression can repay the compliment.

This mutual love in the Godhead between God and God's self-expression, or Word, is called the Holy Spirit. This Spirit can only be Love, for the Spirit of God, who is Love, must also be Love. There is only one God, then, who is Love. But God as Father and God as Word or Son and God as Spirit are not just different names for the same divine being seen in different ways of existing and acting.

This is the assertion of orthodox Christianity: that there is only one God, not three gods, and yet that the Father is God, the Son is God, and the Spirit is God. While the three Persons do not merely share the one divinity among themselves, each of the three Persons is wholly God, nevertheless there is only one God not three, because the three divine Persons are distinct from each other *only* by virtue of the relationships which they have with each other. In other words, there is only one God, but there are three Persons "in" this one God, but only different from each other in the way they relate to each other.

Now here somebody may well impatiently interject: "What is the point of all this very obscure technical theology?" There are two points. First, if Christians were in any way to imply that there were three gods, then the question would immediately arise: "Where do these three gods come from? Must there not be a superior God with a capital "G" (as opposed to god with a small "g") who is the ultimate reality lying behind these three gods?" In which case, we are back to square one: "Who is God?" Second, if God is Love as the New Testament insists and as the whole tradition of Christianity insists, then "Whom does God love?" The obvious answer to that is: the world He created, especially those creatures made in His image. But that only raises the question: What or whom did God love before creation? Was God's love suspended, inoperative until then?

However, there's surely no sense in a God who is Love but who has no one to love from all eternity.

The only subject eternally available for God's love, adequate to and worthy of God's love, must be God and only God. If, then, one believes that love is the most important thing in life, that which alone ultimately makes sense of and gives value to life, and if a personal God is the only kind of God worth believing in, and if therefore this God must above all be a God of love, then the doctrine of the Trinity, mysterious though it be, is actually a doctrine that might almost have had to have been invented if it didn't already exist. If God is Love, then God must have an eternal love-life, if I may use the expression. According to Christianity, this dynamic life of love is eternally active in the relationships of the three Persons of the Trinitarian God.

A monadic as opposed to a Trinitarian God would be a solitary, self-contained deity, who would by no means be naturally open to the idea of creation. A Trinity of three Persons living in a dynamic of love would naturally be creative, overflowing in their love, wanting to share it with created beings. Not to create would surely be against the nature of such a God. There is no question of God being forced to create, but every reason for God wanting to create.

And when one thinks of what sort of creation God would be most interested in, one is forced to conclude that God could only be satisfied by creating creatures as like Himself as possible, only different in not actually being God. After all, a novelist is not content with creating automatons or puppets; the creative novelist wants to create human characters who are real because they seem to be alive with a life of their own. Nothing satisfies a novelist more than when his imagination succeeds in creating a character who does things which the novelist never really consciously intended: the character takes off on its own, as it were, and exists almost independently of the writer.

Now this is how human beings are: utterly dependent on God, and yet sufficiently independent of God to be able even to do things contrary to God's will. For by giving His creatures free will, God gave them their independence. This freedom is obviously not boundless, but it has to be large enough to accommodate love—if God is love and human beings are created in His image. What does that mean?

Well, in human life we wouldn't be interested in compulsory love. For example, we would reject the possibility of forcing someone to like or love us by giving them a pill, which would induce the right sort of feelings. Actually, of course, they couldn't be the right sort of feelings because true liking and love cannot be forced. We might want to make a person behave in a certain kind of way that looked like affection or love, but it wouldn't be the real thing, since the real thing has to come about freely. To like or to love properly involves liking or loving spontaneously and voluntarily. Similarly, if we are intended to love our Creator, the God who is Love, then we can't be forced or programmed to do so; our love, if it is to be genuine love, must be freely given without any sort of compulsion.

But here we have to make an important proviso. If we really *are* created on the model of God, then clearly this ability and desire to love will be natural to us, not something foreign or alien to us, something we have to force ourselves to do when it goes against the grain. If that were the case, then we would have to conclude that God had made a botched job of our creation.

This, then, is the logic of the situation—but what about the facts? And here, of course, we have to admit that in practice we don't, by any means, find it comes easily to love either our fellow human beings or God Himself.

When we were talking about a personal God we came to the conclusion that we should practically have to invent the doctrine of the Trinity for ourselves if we were to follow out the implications of a belief in a genuinely personal God. In the same way, when we consider this glaring contradiction between what it must be our nature to do and our actual failure in practice to do so, we are faced with the inevitability of the Christian doctrines of the Fall and original sin. I mean again that even if these beliefs were not part of the Christian faith, we should be obliged to make them up for ourselves if only to make some sort of sense of the strangely uncomfortable position in which we find ourselves.

And here let us remind ourselves of just how strange it is, although it has become so familiar, so much second nature to us. How easily it comes to our lips to say, by way of excuse for some sinful, that is, unloving, act, "Well, it's only human." Only human? But surely, if we are created to be like our Creator who is Love, then far from being "human," it is most inhuman. In fact, we do use that very word "inhuman" to describe some grossly evil action. We say things like, "only an animal could behave like that." On these occasions we don't hesitate to condemn some terrible crime as inhuman. Why is it that then we use this word so unhesitatingly? And why is it that on other occasions when something wrong, but less wrong, has been done, instead of saying, "That's a bit inhuman, or rather inhuman," we don't hesitate, quite inconsistently, to say, "Oh, it's only human to behave like that?"

The explanation of the contradiction is to be found in the nature of temptation. For it is those things which we are not in the least bit tempted to do that we call "inhuman"—whereas doing those things which we know to be wrong, but which appeal to us, we like to call "only human," as though it were natural for us to do them. I, for example, can honestly say that I have never been tempted to mug an old lady. Now, of course, a mugger might say to me that that is because I am better off than he is and, therefore, am not tempted by the meager contents of the old lady's handbag, but that I would be if I knew there were thousands of dollars in the handbag. And I suppose that if I assured him that even in that case I would not be tempted, he would assume that I was just more self-controlled, more inhibited, less ready to take a risk, than he. But the truth is that most of us, far from being tempted by such an action, would feel extreme repugnance and revulsion if the "temptation" were put before us. The prospect would not just be unappealing, it would be hateful. But there are a great number of other things which I am tempted to do and which I know to be wrong, but which I am inclined to call "only human." However, this behavior which is natural to me is not at all natural to a saint, who would react to my temptations in the same sort of way that I react to the temptations of muggers, rapists, and pedophiles. A saint would rightly regard a good deal of my behavior not just as sinful but as inhuman and unnatural. He or she would rightly be repelled by it. And if I were to conclude that the saint was simply more self-controlled than me, although no less tempted, I would be making a mistake. Not that the saint is perfect. Saints too have their temptations—although probably most of us would regard them as trivial, not worth even noticing, as much a normal part of life as the dust that gathers unseen.

If all sins are inhuman, it follows that the less sinful we are, the more truly human we are. Again, sinful humanity tends to think of the saintly person as somehow inhuman, unnatural, but the reality is the opposite—the holy person is somebody who is more human, more in tune with his nature than the rest of us. Consequently, if a perfect, that is a perfectly loving, person has ever existed or was to exist, that person would be the most really *human* person ever to live in this world.

At this point we should notice something else about such a perfect person, which at first sight might strike us as contradictory. For the most really human of people would also be the most godlike of persons, conforming most closely to the Person in whose image we are created. This may be a surprising thought because we have come to think of the divine and the human as being poles apart. But in reality, the Judeo-Christian tradition doesn't see it at all like that. Far from there being an impassible gulf between the two, the account of creation in the Old Testament sees humanity as created in the image and likeness of the deity. And in the book of Genesis the picture of God walking with the first human beings in the cool of the evening in a hot climate is intended to convey the degree of close intimacy that existed at the beginning between Creator and creatures.

The biblical story goes on to explain how this intimacy was shattered, which, of course, is why we automatically assume that the divine and the human are so separate from each other. But before we consider this catastrophic breakdown, it is worth noting that there has been a long Christian tradition going back to the early centuries which believes that in the divine plan this intimacy was not only intended to persist but to develop to an altogether new intensity. However, in order for this to happen, God would have had to take a new initiative. For although God had created man in His image, the fact remained that God was the maker and man His creation. Could this gulf have been bridged without God ceasing to be the Creator and man the creature?

To understand this attractive speculation which has persisted among Christian thinkers through the ages, let us take as an example the closest parallel to the divine-human relationship that we have in human life, that of the child and the parent. Children like playing, and loving parents like to join in their children's games, but in order to do that they have to come down to the children's level. Indeed, the same is true for any grown-up who wants to make friends with a child. Getting to know a child involves literally coming down to his level, even on all fours. If then God wanted really to communicate with His creatures, He would have had to come down to their level. Like the adult, He would have had to meet us where we are, but like the adult who cannot stop being grown-up, so God cannot cease to be God.

What we are talking about is, of course, the Incarnation. Now it's certainly not an essential part of the Christian or Catholic faith to believe that the Incarnation would have taken place anyway, albeit in a very different way, quite apart from the fatal breakdown in the divine-human relationship which is called the Fall. But this theological speculation does have the merit of emphasizing that God created human beings who were intended to share as far as possible His own divine life. The child-parent analogy again helps here, although, of course, it cannot be exact. After all, parents who lovingly bring children into the world don't want them to stay children forever. They want them to grow up in due course and to share the adult life of the parents, that is, to become grown-ups like their parents, although they will never cease to be the children of their parents. Rather, then, as the children of parents become grown-up children, so God wanted his creatures to become as though they were gods. How, actually, this design had to be carried out was determined by the Fall and the resulting circumstances in which the Incarnation in fact took place.

CHAPTER 3

GOD'S PLAN
FOR THE HUMAN RACE

The two most common objections to Christianity are the problems of evil and pain. Why, it is asked, did God give us free will since He must have known how terribly the human race could or would misuse it? And why would a loving God create a universe that is so full of such dreadful pain and suffering, not all of which can, by any means, be attributed to the evil acts of human beings?

It is easy to understand why unbelievers are so astonished, indeed scandalized, by the obstinacy with which believers persist in believing when the objections seem to them so overwhelming as actually to make honest belief impossible. The difficulties are indeed very serious. But what unbelievers so often don't appear to appreciate is that believers are also amazed, not to say shocked, that there are people who can live their lives in a meaningful and purposeful way and with a sense of moral responsibility, while at the same time refusing to accept that there is any reason to think that this world could have an ultimate cause or purpose, or that this life should have any lasting meaning or significance, or that we will have to render account for the manner in which we live it. We think that people who have no ear for poetry or music, no eye for the visual arts or nature, no palate for food and drink, are the poorer for their deficiency. The religious believer knows that there is such a thing as the spiritual life, not just in theory but in actual practice, to deprive oneself of which is to seriously impoverish one's life.

There are indeed very grave difficulties and objections to religious belief—but are there not even greater problems on the side of unbelief, problems which have a very practical import since each of us has to decide how to live our lives? Fearful suffering presents the believer with an appalling dilemma, but what about the prospect of a life without meaning, a universe that came from nowhere and is going nowhere? It is not obviously irrational to conclude that the latter option is more unreasonable, even absurd.

A further point may be made. What the most common objections to Christianity boil down to is this: the actual fact and nature of existence or creation. Why did God create us as He did, with all the attendant risks? Why did He create the world as it is, with all its very noticeable inconveniences? Why did He not create them differently?

I think two responses can be made to this. First, facts are facts and have to be lived with: this is the life, this is the world we experience—would it not be sensible to behave as if there were a meaning and purpose to it all, especially as we ourselves are people who naturally look for meaning and purpose in our daily lives—who expect to be able to explain how things are? Second, does it make sense to try and imagine a different life, a different world? Can we imagine any other reality except in terms of the reality we experience and know? Do we want a world where there is no hunger or thirst? But then we would have a world in which the pleasures of eating and drinking would not exist. Do we want a world where there is no risk of pain—but then what happens to a virtue like courage? Apart from the physical difficulties of imagining such a world, would not a life and a world without any difficulties or inconveniences negate all or most of the very things that we value? The truth is that when people ask why God could not have created a different world, they are unable to conceive of such a world except in terms of the world they already know. As soon as they try to eradicate the negative elements of life, they find they are also uprooting the positive elements. If we want to complain about the world that has been created, then we have to postulate a world that is quite inconceivable and unimaginable in terms of the human reality which we know and which is the only reality we experience.

If God had not given us free will, He would not have created human beings but automatons. In fact, the dignity and importance of human beings lie in their being able to make choices. Now it is true that our freedom is not complete. We are all influenced by our environments, as well as by the kind of habits that our past actions form. The basic freedom that we all have is the potential capacity to stand back and look at ourselves. We may be severely restricted in our ability to change ourselves and the choices we make, but we can at least criticize our choices, make a moral judgment on our behavior. And this is what, in fact, we do. We deplore many of our choices, however impotent we may be to alter them. We all experience weakness of will, the incapacity to do what we know we ought to do. Nor are these lapses merely exceptions to a general rule of good behavior. There is an innate tendency in all of us toward what we recognize to be evil. It is true that there is also a disposition in us toward good; our orientation is not wholly bad. And yet there is this strange inclination in each of us to prefer evil to good. I say "strange" because, if we are really created in the image of God, we might expect to gravitate naturally in the opposite direction toward our Creator. Something seems to have gone mysteriously wrong. It looks as if human nature, having been originally created to be godlike, has been so radically damaged as to be in a permanently faulty condition. It still bears clear marks of its original condition, but it no longer naturally functions as it was designed to do. Indeed, it seems now to move, if left to its own devices, in a direction the opposite to that of its original orientation.

This pull, which we all feel, is called "original sin," in the Christian view, that is, a critical failure on the part of the human race at the beginning of its history to live up to its God-modeled nature. This original failure has left a kind of permanent scar on human nature, which, although not totally corrupted, is nevertheless seriously damaged and weakened. If we did not possess the story of the Fall of the human race at the beginning of the Bible, we should, as in the case of the Trinity, have practically to invent it. We know the mechanism of what we call human nature is still partly, sporadically working. We can see only too well how it should be working, and yet we can also see that it has been interfered, or tampered with, leaving it only half-working, half-operative.

Because God gave human beings real free will, He had also to grant them the possibility of rejecting Him. If the only love worth having is love freely given, then that choice cannot be forced. If God wants to take us seriously as free human beings, then He must allow us to refuse to love Him. We don't know if any human creature has finally and totally turned his back on God, but logically at least the possibility must be there. This is what is called the doctrine of hell. People are often confused about this, assuming that the doctrine must imply that there are people in the state of hell, but that by no means follows. A condition or state can be hypothetically possible without anyone actually being in it. We just can't know.

The symbolic story told at the beginning of the first book of the Bible graphically illustrates a state of affairs which we all know from unhappy experience. And that is the way in which we choose what is immediately attractive, what appeals to our ego, even though it goes against our conscience and indeed, as we know from bitter experiment in the past, is against our own happiness and interests in the long, if not short, term. The drama of Adam and Eve depicts in universal terms this mad attempt by human beings to prefer themselves to God in defiance of their own created nature and their own good. The friendship and intimacy with their Creator upon which human happiness depends are sacrificed for a suicidal bid to put themselves on a level with God. The great paradox of human sinfulness is that this desperate self-assertion, which leads inexorably to the enslavement of the self, frustrates and prevents God's own desire to raise up His creatures, not out of their creaturely status, which is impossible, but as close to the divine level as is possible for His children.

Original sin, then, consists in the loss of the original holiness with which human beings were endowed on their creation in the likeness of God. This loss leads naturally to a reorientation of the human will. People who are loved find it easier to love than those who are not loved; so long as human beings were ready to be loved by God they found it easy spontaneously to love God and their fellow creatures. When human beings turned their back on God's love, they found that it was no longer easy to love anybody but themselves. No longer looking toward God, they found themselves contemplating the self, and by cultivating their own self they lost their true selves. The Catholic position is, however, that while the human nature which our first ancestors passed on to the whole human race has been seriously damaged, it is not so enslaved to evil as to lose its freedom, not so corrupted as to be completely perverted, as the Protestant Reformers maintained. Here Catholicism agrees with the ordinary human instinct which tells us that as bad as we are in so many ways, we are by no means all bad; we do have good, as well as bad, potential.

The Genesis story, which, we should always remember, is trying to express profound religious truths through images and symbols, imagines Adam and Eve being tempted by a serpent, which is identified in other places in the Bible as the devil or Satan, the chief of the fallen angels. The Christian tradition is that these bodiless spiritual beings are called angels because the word (in Greek) means "messengers." They are messengers, agents of God. Nothing is more calculated to make the unbeliever laugh than the Christian belief in angels, and, of course, many Christians are rather embarrassed by or just dismiss the whole idea. But is the idea so fantastic? After all, if there is a personal God who created and sustains this world, it would not be very surprising if He had the services of lesser created spiritual beings to control the universe and to act as intermediaries between God and His creation. But what of the fallen angels? That may seem an even more fantastic idea. But is it? Doesn't our human experience once again support what the Catholic Christian tradition teaches? Don't we quite naturally speak, in fact, about a spirit of evil? We speak of the presence of evil in places, of evil taking over a person as if the evil comes from outside. Is all this just metaphorical language which we should hate anyone to take literally? I don't think it is. However inexplicable it may be, human experience testifies strongly to the palpable presence of evil in certain situations. Now if there is such a phenomenon, it cannot really be a "thing" at all, since good and evil belong to persons, not things. A thing cannot be evil except as the action of a human being. When we speak of the presence of evil, if we were asked to say if this evil was a person or a thing, I think we would say it was neither—it would be better described as a spirit, in other words a spiritual, but bodiless being—an angel.

Not only, then, is the concept of a fallen or evil spirit true to our experience, but it also helps to explain why, in fact, human beings modeled on God and enjoying intimacy with God could ever have thrown away their good fortune. If evil was not created by them but was already in existence, the problem of evil would be lessened not increased. It might also shed some light on the problem of pain, that is, of suffering which is not inflicted by sinful human beings. If these spiritual agents created by God were also given the same freedom as human beings to choose and if some also used this freedom wrongly, then not only would evil come into existence in the universe, but this unnatural disorder could have had cosmic consequences, such as to produce harmful effects. Certainly, Saint Paul is clear that Christ's entry into the world not only affected the human race but the whole cosmos. We could put it simply by saying that not only is there something wrong with human beings, but all is not well with the world itself. Before human beings sinned, according to Genesis, they were in harmony with the world. For Paul, Christ's Incarnation and redemption were not just for the salvation of the human race, but also for the liberation of the whole world.

All human beings are, by definition, members of the human race. Although we are individuals and belong to different races, there is a unity because we are all human beings sharing the same human nature. When, then, human nature was damaged in the beginning, this had consequences for all of us. And indeed we are ourselves aware that our own sins are not just limited and personal in their effects but help to create an atmosphere or climate which is harmful to our fellow human beings and which also encourages others to sin. Our sins have reverberations and social consequences. The most fundamental of these is that through sin we break the unity of the human race; individuals and groups are divided and set against each other. Through the damage that has been done to our common human nature we incline not to the unity for which we were created but to disunity and disharmony.

If, then, God wanted to release human beings from the consequences of sin, the liberation would have to be both individual and social: that is to say, the remedy would have to be for the race as well as the person. And this is exactly what the Old Testament says: God spoke not just to Moses but through him to a people.

The Jews were not an imperial power like the Romans, nor did they have comparable literary achievements. They certainly did not begin to rival the Greeks in their artistic and intellectual genius. But what they did have, which neither of those two great peoples had, was a deep religious consciousness, expressed through an incomparable body of writings, the Old Testament. Certainly the Greeks and Roman produced no religious literature that can rival theirs.

In the story of Adam and Eve, human beings tragically allow their gaze to drop from God—who should have been their center of attention as the source of their happiness—to their own selves. The human self cut off from its Creator can only be the source of its own misery. Once distracted from what should have been the focus and goal of their affections, human beings naturally begin to lose sight of God.

There is a famous saying of G. K. Chesterton that when people stop believing in God, they don't stop believing; they just start believing in something else. Thus we have the strange spectacle of educated secular Westerners studying horoscopes and the like, not to mention the contemporary idols of health and sex. As soon as human beings allowed their gaze to drop from God, God began to be more dimly seen. Other gods and goddesses representing the elemental forces in a prescientific world seemed to claim human worship if they were to be placated. No doubt the idea of a supreme God above them remained, if only dimly, but there seemed to be spirits and deities more pressingly present who needed appeasing. Polytheism appealed to the fallen mind of a human race no longer enjoying the protective friendship of the Creator and sorely in need of supernatural help. To keep on the right side of the forces that appeared to be in control of the world—whatever might or might not lie behind them—became of paramount importance.

There was, however, one race that differed from the others in retaining, or alternatively in having developed to the point of recovering, the vision of a Creator God. This small Semitic people in the Middle East, of no great political importance, knew they were distinct from their neighbors, and specially privileged, in having this belief in the one God. And not only that. In their treasured sacred literature they expressed the sense that God had chosen them for the unique mission of not only safeguarding this precious knowledge of God, which other peoples had lost through sin, but also of enjoying once again that intimacy with God which had been lost at the Fall. They believed that God had entered into an agreement or contract or sacred treaty with them, whereby He would never abandon them, in spite of the many times they broke the moral commandments He had given to Moses and in spite of their frequent lapses into the idolatry and polytheism that surrounded them on all sides.

According to their religious tradition, God had not given up on the human race after human beings had disrupted their intimacy with Him. At the most fundamental level God continued to communicate with all created beings through their conscience, even though His voice could be more or less successfully muffled. The created world itself continued to suggest to the human mind the existence of a Creator. Their Bible spoke of a contract or covenant that God had originally made with all of humankind after a great flood had threatened to destroy the whole sinful race, whereby He promised that what He had created would be allowed to continue to exist in spite of human sinfulness, although from now on God would accept the disunity of the human race and deal with His creatures separately in their different races and nations. The Old Testament also knows of other great non-Jewish or Gentile figures who were able to recover a considerable degree of intimacy with God.

But it was the Jews who were to enjoy a special relationship with God by being the people chosen to prepare the way for a new unity of the human race divided by sin. Having made this exclusive promise to the race descended from Abraham, God then forged yet another bond with them by giving the moral law to Moses. The later Jewish prophets announced that God intended to make yet another covenant, but this time it would be with the entire human race, who would be offered the chance to be saved through liberation from sin. This new chosen people, therefore, would extend beyond the Jews to all the peoples on the earth.

But if this new human unity was going to come via the first chosen people, we might expect the Jewish religion to yield clues as to the nature of the new People of God and the new religion, that is, the new kind of bond that would bind them to God. The trouble with the morality that God had laid down for the original chosen people was that they found the greatest difficulty in adhering to it. They were in the unfortunate position of knowing far more clearly than their neighbors what they ought to do, but without the means of doing it. This is why the Old Testament is aware that human hearts need to be re-created by some divine Spirit that only God can give. The moral law was there to teach them the nature of their obligations, but what was needed was some divine power that would help their wounded human nature to achieve the necessary motivation to live by it. They had been given tantalizingly, they came to realize, only part of the solution, a true sense of sin but without the power to do much about it. Their so-called prophets began to speak not only of the arrival of a mysterious Spirit that would renew the human heart by writing a new law in it, but also of a liberator, a messianic figure who would possess this Spirit which He would then be able to pass on to others.

The insight into the nature of the one, all-powerful Creator God that set the Jewish people apart from other peoples belonged to them as a nation and race. It was their mission to preserve what had been shown to them *as a people*. The religion and the people went together: what had been shown or revealed to them belonged to them as a people, for they were the chosen People of God. When the messianic liberator came, endowed with the new Spirit, there would be a new People of God which every human being would be invited to join. Presumably, this universal People of God, not limited by racial or national boundaries, would also, like the Jewish people, be the repository of whatever God would reveal through the messianic liberator. In other words, the contents of the new revelation would be entrusted to the safekeeping of the new chosen people, and whatever might be committed to writing would have the same relation to the People of God that the Jewish scriptures had to the chosen people.

What other aspects of Judaism might one expect to have a counterpart in the new People of God? Well, the Jewish religion was certainly more spiritual in its rejection of polytheism and in its strict moral code than any other religion in the ancient world, but that did not stop it from having some very concrete, indeed material elements in it. Like other religions, it had a strong sense of the importance of offering sacrifices, not, however, to the gods but to God. These sacrificial offerings of animals and crops were meant to accompany and express the believer's devotion and worship—otherwise they were seen as empty formalism.

What were these offerings intended to signify? First, the sacrifice was intended as a gift to God to acknowledge the fact that everything created belonged to Him, but the fact that human beings were able to offer back any of God's creation also indicated that God allowed the human use of what He had created. Second, by sacrificing the meat and vegetables that sustain life, the person making the offering could be said to be symbolically surrendering his own life to God, and God, by accepting the offering, could be thought of as accepting this surrender of the person, who was thereby in God's keeping. Destroying the sacrificial offering meant that the animal or vegetable was no longer available for human use and that its disappearance indicated it was now in the invisible sphere of the divine.

There were two other factors. When the part of the offering that was being offered to God had been burned, what remained was eaten by the person or persons making the offering, thereby establishing a kind of spiritual communion between God and the offerer through partaking of the same animal or vegetable. Finally, there was always some element of expiation, since making such a sacrifice also involved a sacrifice in the sense of self-denial.

There was one religious feast in the Jewish year that took precedence over all the others and that was the Passover, the annual commemoration of the liberation of the Jews from slavery in Egypt. This sacred meal, at which roast lamb and unleavened bread (indicating the haste in which the Jews fled) were eaten, was—and is—a family celebration of the passing from Egyptian bondage to freedom in the land "flowing with milk and honey," the land of Canaan. At the heart of the celebration, then, was a definite historical event carefully retained in the collective memory of the Jewish people.

CHAPTER 4

A SPECIAL PEOPLE

In the Gospels, when Jesus comes out on the public stage, He begins by calling on His fellow Jews to repent as "the kingdom of heaven" is at hand. Through this message or proclamation He both asserts the unique mission of the Jewish people and also hints at the new chosen people which will emerge from this nucleus. The sovereignty of God over the chosen people is to be extended over the whole world by means of the race which acknowledges the one Creator God as no other religion does.

But this announcement is immediately followed by Jesus' calling upon certain men to be His associates in His campaign to rouse the Jews to a fresh realization of their destiny. This campaign, however, will not take the form of a nationalist rising against the occupying Roman power, as was commonly expected, but of a purely spiritual movement. It could easily strike anyone reading the Gospels for the first time without any Christian preconceptions (but not someone who was brought up with the idea that Christianity comes into the world through the Bible), that the gospel writers never make any claim that their memoirs of Jesus were suggested, let alone ordered, by Jesus Himself.

This is surely a remarkable fact. After all, the writers were very conscious of the enormously important task they had set themselves, and nothing could have been more affirming than to be able to claim that they were only carrying out Jesus Christ's own instructions to them. But that brings us to another interesting fact. For not only do the Gospels contain not the trace of a hint that any of Jesus' doings and sayings were to be recorded in writing, but there is no evidence at all that anyone took notes at the time. And again, it would have been very useful to the gospel writers to establish the authenticity of their accounts if they could have claimed to be basing their narratives on records made at the time. But far from that, there is not a sign of anyone in the Gospels ever writing anything, with one striking exception. In the famous story of the woman caught in adultery, Jesus is reminded that the Jewish law prescribed execution for this moral transgression. It is a trap, of course, since, if the forgiveness and mercy of God, which is at the heart of His revolutionary teaching, means anything, then He can hardly endorse the law's severity. Faced with this dilemma, Jesus, we are told, mysteriously starts to write on the ground with His finger, before issuing His challenge to anyone there who has never sinned to throw the first of the stones, as prescribed by the Jewish law. The gospel writer doesn't tell us what Jesus wrote; presumably he didn't know. Nor does he throw any light on this enigmatic gesture. But it is certain that the only time Jesus is recorded as having written anything was in this entirely casual and informal way; it was writing that was not intended to last beyond the immediate moment.

Perhaps even more startling is what took place, or rather didn't take place, on the night before Jesus' execution. It's clear from all the accounts that Jesus was perfectly aware that the moment His enemies had been looking for had come. Both His work and His life were now about to end. Anyone facing execution naturally wants to be able to see those closest to him in his last hours. He wants to leave messages, or make a last will and testament if he has not already prepared one. On that fateful night, there was not a lot of time for Jesus to ensure that His disciples had the fullest possible instructions on how they were to continue His mission. In particular, it would have helped enormously, one would have thought, if Jesus had Himself composed a New Testament. It was not as if there had not been enough time before to do this. We know that Jesus took a long time to even begin His public work—He was already into His thirties. Again, the Gospels record many occasions when Jesus went away to be by Himself. It is true that it was to pray to His Father, as He called God. But, noticeably, there never appeared to be any hurry or rush;

there seemed to be all the time in the world. There is a complete lack of any program of action or schedule of things that had to be done. Miraculous cures are worked and teachings enunciated, but on no apparent plan or policy. They seem to happen quite by chance as circumstances called for them. In the absence of anything that could remotely be called frenzied activism, one might have thought that Jesus could easily have spent more, not less, time by Himself, and taken the trouble to write down what was left to the New Testament writers to write down. He could surely have presented at least the teaching far more systematically and thoroughly. Those Christians, for example, who claim that they get their beliefs from the Bible as opposed to any church, might reasonably have expected to find the central Protestant doctrine of justification by faith alone categorically and specifically stated by Jesus. If one thinks that everything depends on the written Scriptures, it is hard not to convict Jesus of a certain willful negligence. It is not as if He was some unlettered teacher; He could certainly read and write as the Gospels make plain. If Jesus' message and mission were intended to be carried on and propagated by means of written texts, it is hard not to conclude that the job was strangely botched.

Fortunately, there is, of course, another way altogether of seeing the relation between the New Testament and the life and work of Jesus. And that is to appreciate the parallel to the relation between the Old Testament and the original chosen People of God. Judaism, after all, was far from being a purely "Scriptural" religion. The original covenant or agreement between God and the father of the Jewish people, Abraham, was not signified by writing but was literally stamped on the bodies of Jewish males through physical circumcision. It is certainly true that the revelation of God's commandments to Moses was later put into writing, just as the reading of the Scriptures in the synagogue was a major part of the Jewish religion, as were the teachers or interpreters of the law, the Scribes and the Pharisees. In addition, there were the priests, the temple in Jerusalem where sacrifices were offered, and the major feasts like the Passover, which were celebrated in the home.

If we turn to the New Testament and the new People of God, it is perfectly clear that the New Testament did not precede but, rather, came after the Church. Eventually, the Church had to decide which were the authentic, "inspired" Scriptures. Indeed, the writers of the New Testament books were, of course, Christians or members of the new People of God before they ever put pen to paper. In other words, both in the case of the Old Testament and the New Testament, the People of God, or the Church, comes before the written texts which are produced by certain of its members and authenticated by its leaders.

If we look at Jesus' life, we find that He was not only a teacher or "rabbi," whose words could be committed to writing, but that He also *did* things. First and foremost, after His initial proclamation of the "good news," He picked twelve men to be His immediate associates and helpers in announcing and furthering God's rule in the new era that was opening. Then He not only worked a great number of miraculous healings, but, more interestingly, while He repeatedly said that these cures depended on people having faith, He also didn't hesitate to use material things. On one occasion, for example, He cured a blind man not by words but by spitting on the ground and making a paste with the spittle, which He applied to the man's eyes. This mysterious teacher and miracle-worker by no means relied only on words. There was a strange earthiness attached to much of what He did, which sits uncomfortably with any concept of a religion bound up exclusively with the written word of the Bible. Indeed, the first miracle the Gospels record is the turning of water into wine at a wedding reception, the religious point of which is not immediately obvious. Its significance becomes clearer when Jesus is later reported as saying that He is the "living bread" which has come down from heaven, recalling for His Jewish listeners the strange food called "manna" that mysteriously appeared in the desert to sustain the Jews after they had escaped from Egypt. This living bread, He adds, is His "flesh," and not only does this new spiritual life that Jesus is offering depend upon eating the bread of His Flesh, but those who wish to have real life, followed by eternal life, must also drink His Blood, which is "drink indeed" as His flesh is "food indeed" (John 6:55).

Not surprisingly, the Gospel, which records this strangely materialistic, even apparently cannibalistic, statement, goes on to mention that this "intolerable language" put off a lot of His hearers for good. But, significantly, Jesus makes no effort to gloss it over by explaining that He was only speaking metaphorically not literally—although He does make it clear that His words are not intended in an actual carnal sense. The import of His mysterious words must have become a great deal clearer to His closest associates when, on the night before He was executed, He did something quite extraordinary at their last meal together. So far as they were concerned, they had come together to celebrate the Passover meal. The custom was to begin with a first course, and then for the father of the household solemnly to bless the bread and the wine on the table. But when Jesus came to this important moment in this greatest of Jewish feasts, He did something that was not only extremely odd, but, given the occasion, something that might have seemed the height of blasphemy. According to the Gospels, He took the bread and the wine and, after saying the traditional blessing, proceeded to make a very mysterious announcement to the effect that the bread He had just blessed was His Body which they were to eat, and then that they should drink the wine He had just blessed, "for this is my blood." He then gives His disciples, who were no doubt quite bewildered, this explanation: namely, that the Blood, His Blood, belonged to what he called "the covenant," which was to be "poured out for the forgiveness of sins." His hearers did not need to be very devout or instructed Jews to pick up the allusion. It was clearly to the "covenant," that is, the formal agreement or contract entered into by God on the one side and the chosen People of God on the other, in other words, the very foundation of the whole Jewish faith. This solemn pact, whereby God made certain promises to the privileged race in return for an undertaking by the Jews to observe His moral law, was ratified at Mount Sinai when Moses sprinkled half the blood from an animal sacrifice on an altar representing God and the other half on the people themselves.

Jesus' intention here at the Last Supper was clear enough to any Jew. He was introducing a completely new sacrifice to ratify a new contract between God and the human race. Instead of the blood of an animal, henceforward it was to be human blood that was to bind the two parties together. But what sort of human blood was this wine over which such mysterious words had been uttered? And what about the bread which had also been singled out in a similar

Chapter 5

Getting under Our Skin

Catholic Christianity believes that the identity of Jesus Christ is similar to the nature of God in the sense that both are mysteries which are beyond full human understanding. Just as God is one and yet three persons, so Jesus is both divine and human at the same time. And not partly divine and partly human, but fully and truly God and fully and truly human.

The mystery, however, will appear less impenetrable if we recall that humanity is made in the image or likeness of God, so that the more really human a person is, the closer he or she will resemble God. In other words, the most human of people will also be the most godlike of people. The more we are in harmony with our real human nature, the more we shall be like God. If, then, there ever existed a human being who was totally in accord with human nature as God intended it to be, that is, like to God, then that person will also presumably be the most nearly divine of human beings. As we have said, to place the human in opposition to the divine is not in accordance with God's plan. The two are meant to be closely conjoined.

The orthodox Christian view is that Jesus is the only perfect human being who has ever existed. But if so, then He is also the nearest of all people who have ever existed to being God. When we think about it in that way, we begin to see that the idea of someone being both God and man is not, after all, quite so baffling.

We have already seen that if God wanted to communicate in an intimate way with the human race, He would have to come down to our level, to meet us on our level. That is one reason for the Incarnation. But there are other reasons why God adopted our human nature. The only really effective way, after all, in which He could show us how much He loves us would be to show His love in a human way. To prove and make real His love for us, God would have to put on a human face, so to speak. His love for us would have to be manifested in a mode and terms that we could both experience and understand. Since giving up one's own life to rescue somebody else is considered the highest possible form of love, the supreme self-sacrifice, then if God were able to do this—and He would have to do it as a human being—He would express His infinite love for His creatures in a way to which they could immediately respond.

But there was another reason for the Incarnation. It is perhaps the most profound reason, but a reason which is sadly and strangely neglected, even unknown, although it was very familiar to the great teachers of the early Church—the Fathers, who expounded Catholic Christianity in the centuries that followed the age when the New Testament was composed.

The Incarnation was not simply a matter of God coming down to join us on our level, but also of drawing us up to His level. To take again the analogy of the child and the adult, a grown-up who plays with a toddler on the ground is both coming down to the level of the toddler and, by so condescending, is allowing the child to have a real personal contact with the adult world. Perhaps a clearer example would be that of a parent who takes his adolescent son or daughter for the first time into their confidence, treating him or her for the first time as an adult. By so doing, the parent enables the child to share in experiences which were previously known, if at all, only by second-hand or in theory.

The Fathers called this aspect of the Incarnation the deification or divinization of human nature. But, as we have already seen, human analogies break down because a grown-up cannot actually become a child or a parent his teenage son or daughter. But in the unique case of the Incarnation, God doesn't just come down to our level in an external and momentary kind of way. It's true He doesn't cease to be God—if He did there would be no point in the exercise—but He does truly become human. He doesn't dress up in a sort of disguise, pretending to be human while actually still staying God, as we do when we impersonate somebody. No, God truly comes down to us because He really takes on our human nature, but He also at the same time, by doing so, draws us up into His life because He doesn't cease to be God.

If we were to watch an actor or actress playing us on the stage or screen—as can happen to famous people—we may feel our privacy is being invaded, especially if the impersonation is a good one, but we certainly don't feel that our own character or personality has somehow been radically altered by what takes place. To impersonate or play someone is not really to change him in any real way—although, of course, it may change the public perception of that person for good or for bad—but if somebody could actually *become* somebody else, presumably that would be a different matter. In that case a person would not just feel his privacy had been invaded, he would feel that his very person was being invaded. But that is what happened to humanity at the Incarnation.

For it was not only that God underwent what we can only call an experience in taking our human nature, but that human nature could not have that happening to it without a radical effect on its makeup. This isn't something that is easy to explain or understand, but it would be as if we could get right into somebody else and experience exactly what it is like to be that person, to have his feelings and his thoughts. It's not something, of course, that can ever literally happen, but it's not impossible in a way to imagine it. In fact, we have an interesting expression to indicate our reaction to somebody intruding in an unwelcome way into our life when we say that so-and-so "is getting under my skin." We don't have such a concrete and graphic expression to mean the same thing when it is a pleasant, positive experience. We can only then use the much less physical idea of somebody "empathizing" with us, that is, to recall the Greek meaning of the word, "suffering" or "experiencing" what we suffer or experience. There is, though, the more vivid visual expression of "seeing" right into somebody.

Well, in the Incarnation God does indeed not only empathize with or see into us, but, in the most positive sense, gets under our very skin. He does that by not only literally putting on our human skin, but by putting on all that is part and parcel of being a human person. There is one exception to that, although, as we have already seen, it is not really an exception at all. I am referring, of course, to the fact that the one thing God doesn't take to Himself, and can't, unless He were to cease to be God, is sin. But since sin is inhuman rather than human, by sinning the Incarnate God would make Himself less not more human.

If indeed God got into our very skin at the Incarnation, then human nature could never be the same again. It had not only been brought close to divinity, but it had actually been penetrated and impregnated by God. In that case, human nature had now entered into an even more elevated state than the original condition of innocence of sin, since Adam and Eve are depicted as enjoying close friendship and intimacy with God, but with a God who still remains apart and distinct. Through God becoming human in Jesus Christ, human nature receives an extraordinary, radical injection of new, that is, divine life. Human nature, created to be like God, now finds itself invaded by its Creator. When people emigrate to another country and another culture they inevitably have an effect on that society; there is now a new element or ingredient which more or less alters the scene. When God decided to enter the human race, He could not but change the humanity He adopted. Of course, sin remained in the race, and so from that point of view there was still loss rather than gain compared with the original sinlessness of the first creatures. But there was a revolutionary gain, too.

An analogy may help to make this clear. Somebody who has been injured may never recover from his wounds, never quite be healed. But suppose that person goes to a new climate and a new environment, which enormously benefits his general health. The old wounds may still cause trouble, still flare up and hurt, but everything else takes on a new look. His whole health so improves that now he is capable of things he couldn't do before. He sleeps better than ever before. He is capable of physical exertion, which was beyond his strength even before he was wounded. No, those wounds will never go away, never cease to aggravate, and may actually cause further complications—nevertheless, that person's family and friends marvel at how he has become "a new person." Those who knew him before exclaim, "I wouldn't have recognized him, he looks so well!" Nothing has changed in the one aspect, what originally caused him to go abroad, but otherwise everything else has changed immeasurably for the better. That person might even say, "I now see that those injuries which seemed to spell the loss of health, even life itself, turned out to have been a blessing in disguise. If it hadn't been for that terrible accident, I would never have moved to a better climate which has given me a totally new lease on life."

This is what came about through the Incarnation. The old human nature remained, sinful and weak. But now there was new hope, altogether fresh possibilities. It was not that the damage that had been done was removed with a wave of a wand. That remained—nothing could change what had so tragically happened. And yet everything could change. Like the injured person carrying his disabilities for life but given a new life immensely better than anything he had ever known even before the terrible accident—so now the human race was renewed in a way that would have seemed inconceivable even in the original state of innocence. It was not just that disabled human nature was given hope that one day things would be all right. Now real possibilities opened up. Human nature suddenly found itself capable of things undreamed of before.

I said just now that the Word of God did not merely put on a human disguise to pretend to be a human being. When I also said that the Incarnate God actually got under our skin, I certainly wasn't only talking metaphorically. For, of course, it wasn't only our human nature in a purely mental sense that Jesus took onboard. Nor did He put on a human skin, take to Himself a human body as a sort of instrument so as to adopt a human nature. No, the body was as important and integral a part of His humanity as it is of ours.

I stress this because there have been self-professed Christians who have—understandably in view of the disgusting and sordid things that human beings are capable of doing with their bodies—been tempted to downgrade or dismiss the human body as, at best, an irrelevance, at worst a serious hindrance to the real spiritual identity of human beings. But that has never been the Catholic approach. The first miracle Jesus is supposed to have worked would otherwise be highly frivolous, to say the least. Given the terrible things that human beings are inclined to do when intoxicated, it is certainly tempting to regard wine, for example, as something intrinsically evil to be avoided at all costs. According to the Gospels, Jesus took no such line. Indeed, the very opposite, since wine plays such a significant role at both the beginning and the end of His mission.

This is because wine is intrinsically good not bad, because it is part of God's creation, intended for the sustenance and indeed enjoyment of human beings—whatever bad uses they may put it to because of their tendency to spoil God's creation. The same is true of the human body: it was created by God. But there is more to it than that. The fact is that we can't imagine, as we have never experienced what it would be like, to be purely spirit and no body. And yet there are people, who profess to be Christians, who regard the body, it seems, rather as a maimed person would regard the loss of a limb, say a hand. The loss is inconvenient but it's not essential to life, although the hand is a very useful instrument to have, one can still live without it. Now, as I say, some people appear to think of the whole body like that—as though it were just a sort of glorified instrument for the human spirit to use on this earth.

But medical science, not to say ordinary common sense, doesn't support that way of looking at the human person. We know that the body is not at all like a walking stick or an umbrella, which are useful but quite external to us. Things like that, however useful or even necessary, are not part of us—but the body is. We act and exist as an indivisible whole. If a part of our brain ceases to function, that affects how we think. When we feel nervous or afraid or embarrassed, we don't register the fact by deliberately deciding to have butterflies in our tummy or goose-pimples on our flesh or blushes on our cheeks—as we might wave a flag exultantly to show our joy or a gun menacingly to register our terror. No, these physical manifestations just happen, even against our will. Our bodies are in tune because they are inextricably linked to our feelings and thoughts. There is no escape from our bodies in this life.

When, then, God decided to come down to our level it was necessary for Him to literally "get under our skin." It would not have been enough for Him to have had a purely spiritual presence by appearing as a glorified angel, for instance. Nor would it have been enough for the spiritual manifestation to have been contained or embodied in some apparent but not real body. For the Incarnation to take place it was necessary for God, that is, His Word, to take physically our flesh and bones. Had He not done that, He would not have been properly and fully human. His coming down to our level, His bringing the divine into union with the human, would only have partially, incompletely been accomplished. No, if God wanted literally to join His creation, the human race, He had to do just that.

If God was simply the all-powerful source of the universe, there would no doubt be something shocking, scandalous, even blasphemous about such an idea. That, of course, is exactly how it struck many people at the time. Indeed, it would be hard to see the point in it. Why, after all, should God condescend to the human level? By doing so, would he not in effect be lowering Himself, demeaning His divine authority?

For the Word, or Son of God, to carry out His mission of teaching about the Creator to the human race, it was entirely appropriate that He should communicate with human beings on their own level. The message, like all messages, depended greatly on the messenger. God, the Jews believed, had sent plenty of messengers in the past. Sometimes He had done so directly through strange and mysterious manifestations. Much more often, it was indirectly through people He had inspired, called prophets by the Jews. God might even have appeared on very rare occasions under human form, but the Jews knew that was not real: it was a disguise by which God could make direct and intelligible contact. But all that was quite different from God delivering His message in His own person—in the actuality of a human person with a real human nature. If God really had done that, then one could see why. That way, the message took on not only a new potency and urgency, but an altogether new tone and force. The slogan, "the medium is the message," makes the point. A distant, transcendent God might tell human beings that love was the key to the universe, but how differently that message would come across if God Himself delivered the message by coming among human beings as a real human being Himself, who could express this love not only in human words but in human actions and behavior. After all, as the old saying has it, actions speak louder than words.

CHAPTER 6

GOD'S EXPERIENCE OF DEATH

Part of human life, that is, the end of human life, is death. It is an inescapable ingredient of the human experience, although it only happens once to each of us. But obviously it colors, or rather shadows, the life which precedes it. All our other experiences are affected by the fact that we know that all this experience will end sooner or later. It is a truism that the day we are born is a day closer to death. Because we have no experience of what, if anything, happens after death, our feelings about it are different from all the other feelings we have about our experiences. It is the great unknown which we approach in complete ignorance and normally in greater or lesser trepidation. We also know that while death can come suddenly without our experiencing any pain, it can also, and usually is, preceded by the aches and ailments of old age and often by severe bodily suffering.

In its symbolic account of creation and the Fall, the Bible indicates the original happiness and innocence of human beings by imagining a garden or oasis in the midst of a desert, an image that belongs to the Middle Eastern world. It pictures God walking in the cool of the evening, which, apart from the early morning, is the best time of the day in a hot country for people to take a stroll with their friends and loved ones. God finds that the creatures He has created hide from Him. They are no longer able to stroll in closeness and intimacy with their Creator. God is depicted as immediately knowing what has happened to break their friendship. They have obviously eaten the fruit of the so-called tree of the knowledge of good and evil. Again, this is a symbol the biblical writer uses to signify the power of deciding for oneself what is good and evil and of behaving accordingly. The forbidden fruit represents a moral autonomy which denies the created status of human beings. It is an act of rebellion against the sovereignty of God, arising out of the capital sin of pride. In the story God had warned Adam and Eve that if they did taste the fruit of that tree they would certainly die.

What would have happened to the first created beings, if they had never sinned, is not revealed in the story. But since God intended His human creation to enjoy with Him His divine life, we are not required to believe that Adam and Eve would have lived an eternal earthly life. That would rule out the elevation of humanity to the Godhead and the intended union of the divine and human. However, what we can say is that the kind of death that now faced Adam and Eve and their descendents was not originally intended by God at all. That doesn't mean it was an arbitrary act on God's part. Rather, it was the inevitable consequence of choosing to go their own way independently of God that ensured that created beings would return to the dust from which, in the biblical account, God had created them. To put it in another way, by deciding to act as though they were God, human beings ended up rejecting their subordinate relationship to God and, thereby, their own identity which lay in their being created in God's image. Once human beings no longer wanted to be in the image of God, they effectively denied that they were created at all. And by rejecting their creation they undid what God had done and returned to the uncreated state of non-existence. Actually, in fact, they couldn't literally do that because they had been created for immortality. Still, they were able to disrupt their nature to such an extent that they forfeited spiritual control over their bodies.

Their physical existence had been critically affected—but so had their attitude to the end of their earthly existence. Because human beings no longer enjoyed friendship and intimacy with God, death became a source of the dread of the unknown. Alienation from their Creator meant that the termination of physical existence was not automatically welcomed as signifying union with God. Death meant not only physical suffering but mental and spiritual anguish.

If God were to lower Himself to the level of humanity and to participate in the whole of human life, it was necessary that He too should experience death. The only difference was that God could not actually Himself sin—but that didn't mean that He couldn't suffer the consequences of sin.

To appreciate this gives us a fuller understanding of the accounts we have of Christ's death. Crucifixion was the cruelest form of capital punishment practiced by the Romans. It was never inflicted on Roman citizens, but used for slaves and rebels. The Roman governor Pontius Pilate had no choice but to order such an execution in the face of the treasonable charge that Jesus had proclaimed Himself the king of the Jews. In a crucifixion, death came through asphyxiation, a drawn-out process, accentuating the torment. But one of the gospel writers records that Pilate was astonished that Jesus died so quickly (see Mark 15:44). This suggests that there is a particular significance in Jesus' final words from the Cross, in which, according to the different gospel accounts, He cried out: "My God, my God, why have you deserted me?" "Father, into your hands I commit my spirit," and "It is accomplished." The anguish of the first is generally contrasted with the deliberate calmness of the last two, but there need not be any contradiction. The fact that Jesus died prematurely suggests that He might not have died of asphyxiation but of something else. In that case, it is plausible to think that Jesus chose His moment to suffer whatever killed Him. After all, He had publicly said that He had the power to lay down His life—suggesting that He would choose that moment—and certainly when death did come, it was accepted with majestic calm.

Now although Jesus could not Himself sin, the New Testament is adamant that He took the sins of the world on Himself. Well, suppose He did do that quite literally. That is to say, He experienced sin but without actually Himself sinning. For the Word of the God, who is Love, to endure that alienation from God which is the essence of sin, must surely be of a horrific nature such as we can only dimly glimpse in our own easy familiarity both with sin and its consequences and effects. Indeed, for Jesus to suffer separation from the Father, which is what sin involves, would be nothing other than death itself. If this is so, then we can bring together the two different cries that the Gospels report: Jesus brings death on Himself by submitting to the ultimate of all suffering—the experience of the condition of sin. We could put it another way by saying that Jesus chose the moment when He would allow His heart to be broken by feeling that sense of abandonment which is the lot of fallen humanity. When Jesus had experienced that, He had experienced the fullness of the human condition and had endured a mental and spiritual pain far in excess of the bodily pain of execution. Just as human beings experience physical pain in a way an animal, which doesn't have self-awareness, cannot do, so God the Son endured a suffering which is incommensurate with any suffering known to human beings when in His humanity He felt what it is like to be alienated from God. And so Jesus chose the moment when He permitted that separation which for Him meant instant death. For one endless moment He plumbed the very depths of human misery.

In dying, then, Jesus not only completed His experience of the whole gamut of human life, but by the manner of His death, He also participated in that sense of abandonment and alienation which is at the heart of human suffering and fear of death. His cry of desolation, "My God, my God, why have you deserted me?" is usually regarded as a cry of distress but not despair, since it is a quotation from one of the psalms which is followed by an expression of joyful confidence in final victory. Certainly, Jesus knew His Jewish scriptures, to which He frequently referred, and expected His hearers to pick up the allusions. But the fact that He is quoting from this psalm does not exclude the possibility that He uses the familiar words as an expression of His own agony and that this agony is not simply the physical agony of crucifixion but, far more profoundly, the agony of experiencing what it is for human beings to be alienated from their Creator. For one moment Jesus allows, as His final sacrifice, that absolute intimacy between His Father and Him, which is so often on His lips in the Gospels, to be shattered. This helps to explain the agony in the garden of Gethsemane when Jesus prays, "Take this cup away from me," "My Father, if it is possible, let this cup pass me by." The distress, indeed anguish ("his sweat became like great drops of blood falling upon the ground" [Luke 22:44]), that the Gospels record, surely indicate something much more terrible than even terrible physical pain. Physical pain is not something which the Jesus who is portrayed in the Gospels would have shrunk from. Nor would death hold any terror for Jesus who knew His Father would never abandon Him. The only thing that could really have horrified Jesus, apart from actually sinning, would have been to take the sin of the world on Himself by experiencing what it would be like to be no longer in deep communion with His Father, to suffer the dreadful ordeal, however momentarily, of alienation and distance from the source of His divinity.

But Jesus' death involved more than the fulfillment of His Incarnation, the ultimate solidarity with fallen human nature. For the New Testament insists that Jesus' death was redemptive, a ransom for the human race, on behalf of every member for whom Jesus offered His life. He Himself had already taught that there is no greater act of love than to lay down one's life for somebody else. He now lays down His life for everyone who has ever lived and will live. In the place of an animal sacrifice offered to God by way of compensating or paying for human sin, Jesus offers Himself. This is more than a human sacrifice, for Jesus is the incarnate Son of God. In order to come down to our level so as to raise us up to His level, God had to join the human race. It was not as if God said to Himself "If you can't beat them, join them"—but rather, "If you can't change them, join them." In order to offer the only sacrifice that could really make up for human sin, God had to offer Himself. The blood with which this new agreement or contract was signed was no longer with the blood of an animal: it was the blood of the incarnate Son of God. His self-sacrifice is uniquely effective because it is done with the love of which only God is capable. Love itself cancels out all the suicidal self-love of the human race and inaugurates a fresh beginning, a new relationship between the Creator and His creatures.

Jesus' acceptance of death, the ultimate self-sacrifice of love, is the consummation of His life and work. It is the supreme example of all His teaching about the meaning and purpose of life. But the New Testament insists that there is more to the crucifixion than that. For by dying on the Cross, Jesus frees us from the consequences of our sinful self-assertion and offers us the forgiveness of God. The power of sin and death over the human race is destroyed.

We have already seen that while Jesus could not Himself sin without ceasing to be God (and for that matter the most human of all human beings, a being without that most inhuman of things, sin), that didn't mean He couldn't experience what it is like to sin, what it feels like to be alienated and cut off from the source of life. By entering into the depth of human experience, Jesus on the Cross puts Himself in our suicidal place. He understands finally what it feels like to be a sinner. At last He drinks the full cup of human misery, the cup that even He begged the Father that He should not have to drink. No one now can say that Jesus, being God, didn't really know what it is to be a human being. By this supreme act of solidarity, Jesus shares, as it were, in the terrible consequences of the Fall. And by so doing, He brings a new element, the divine, into the tragic situation. The human tragedy can never be quite the same again. God's very presence has altered it. Without, of course, taking sin into the Godhead—an impossibility—the Son of God brings the human experience of separation from God into the purview, as it were, of God. The sense of alienation which is at the heart of human despair is no longer strange and external to God. We can hardly say that God blesses the experience, or waves a wand to dispel it, but we can surely say that He lays a healing hand on it.

Mothers say to their small children when they've hurt themselves, "I'll kiss it and make it better." By this they mean that they can't get rid of the cut or the bruise, but they can, by touching it with their lips, somehow lovingly share in it and thus make the pain less. The wound continues to hurt in exactly the same physical way as before, but now its power to distress and frighten is lessened. In a similar sort of way, by experiencing what Jesus does at the very end, He transforms the pain. The human sense of alienation will no longer feel the same. God knows about it, has endured it, and this sense of solidarity makes all the difference. Everything remains the same and yet everything has changed. Sin has lost its stranglehold because its power to produce absolute despair has been taken away from it: God sympathizes, that is, in the original meaning of the Greek word, suffers with us, and that gives us hope. For sympathy has its own capacity to remove pain and suffering.

Jesus, at the crucifixion, gave us the perfect model of that self-sacrificing love which He had taught was the key to the meaning of life and to human happiness. He also led the way, as the head of the new liberated human race, in confronting and enduring the agony of the human condition, so that human beings could accept suffering and death in a wholly new way. But neither of these points, important as they are, explains how Jesus' death on the Cross can be what is called in theology the "atonement" for sin. How does God the Son by suffering death in His human nature conciliate God the Father and liberate the human race from sin? What is this reconciliation between God and humankind supposed to be? There have been various theological theories to explain what the New Testament means by saying that Jesus' death takes away the sin of the world by propitiating God and reconciling God with the human race, bringing about an *at-one-ment* between the two. But perhaps the theory that makes most sense today is the one that emphasizes the aspect of ransom.

We all understand what it means when a kidnapper asks for a ransom. It usually means that the kidnapped person will be released on the payment of a sum of money. Alternatively, the victim may be a hostage who will only be released if the political demands of the terrorists involved are met. Or it may be that the kidnappers are only interested in exchanging their prisoner for the release of certain prisoners associated with their cause. Well, on the Cross Jesus, in effect, offers Himself to God in our place. We are the sinners who deserve to die because of our sins, but Jesus accepts the punishment on our behalf. "Kill me and not my son," a distraught mother may beg her son's captors. This is what Jesus says to the Father on the Cross—"Let me be killed not them." He not only stands where we should be, He pays the only ransom that can equal and surpass the cost of human sinfulness. The negative value of the sin of the world is so colossal that the only thing that can meet the cost is the blood of the incarnate Son of God. Nothing else can wipe out the horrendous debt which the ruined race has run up and still runs up.

To this it might be objected: surely God who is all-powerful could simply cancel the debt, announce that it no longer counted, and He would simply overlook it. Two answers can be made to this. First, God is certainly all-powerful but He is also all-just. To ignore sin, as though it were not there, would be an act of mercy but not of justice. By paying the price Himself, God displays both justice and mercy. Second, because God created us as He did, giving us free will and paying us the enormous compliment of making us like Him, He has to take us very seriously indeed, including our sinfulness. Sin is something very real and we are responsible for it. Nothing could illustrate more profoundly its terrible reality than God Himself taking it upon Himself to tackle it head-on. It can't just be waved away as though it didn't really exist.

Furthermore, we need to remember the spiritual forces or powers in the world. If evil exists as a principle or spirit and not just the evil actions of human beings, then there is only one adversary who is really capable of decisively defeating it, and indeed only one opponent that the spirit of evil would really want to overcome. On that Good Friday this spirit or Satan or the devil had at last the only prey really worth having in his grasp. But in such a struggle there could only be one outcome. God the Creator could not be overpowered by a spirit created by God. In this most direct and immediate encounter of good and evil, which is only the negative absence and denial of good, since everything is created by the Creator who cannot create what is not good, God who is Love shows who is in command and who must always be the victor in any ultimate conflict.

CHAPTER 7

THE IMPORTANCE OF THE BODY

At death, life leaves our body, which then ceases to function. If we are, in fact, spiritual as well as corporeal beings and if we are created to live on after physical death, then presumably that which makes up our spiritual life continues to somehow exist. It is this part of us, although, of course, it is not a part of us like our neck is part of our body, which is traditionally called the soul. When Jesus experienced death in His humanity, then His physical body also ceased to have life in it. But His human soul, like ours, continued to exist, although separately from His dead body. The big difference from us was that He possessed a divine as well as human nature, which meant that neither His human body nor His soul could be separated from the divine person of Christ. Divinity continued to exist in both human components, so that the division between body and soul, which takes place at death, and which constitutes death, could not persist in the case of the God-man. It is this reunion of the two components or parts of the man Jesus that came apart at death which is what is meant by the Resurrection.

Now it is important to stress that resurrection is not the same as resuscitation. The Gospels record how Jesus Himself brought three dead people back to life, that is, earthly life, but death was only postponed till sometime in the future. This was, however, not the case with Jesus. He was not merely returning miraculously to ordinary life on this earth, nor was He destined to die again. It is true that after the Resurrection, His disciples were left in no doubt that what they were seeing was no ghost. What they saw with their eyes was confirmed by a body, which they could not only touch but which could partake of a meal with them. Moreover, by displaying the wounds inflicted by the crucifixion, this body was shown to be the same body that had belonged to Jesus.

There is, however, a critical difference which reveals the absolute difference between resuscitation and resurrection. Although the body the disciples saw and touched seemed clearly to be Jesus' body, there was something very mysterious, very strange about this body. This body was not necessarily immediately recognized by His close associates, although Jesus had only very recently died. Sometimes something was needed to trigger recognition: sometimes Jesus appeared under one form, sometimes under another. Nor was His body limited as before by space and time. It was the same body as before, and yet it was not the same body. And, of course, the reason is quite simple: Jesus had come back to life, but heavenly not earthly life. At this point one might ask: "Was the body, then, that appeared to the disciples not real at all, but just a temporary sort of body which Jesus donned so He could show His disciples that He really had been freed from death and was once again alive, albeit now with a divine life only?" In other words, had Jesus' bodily life come to an end at His crucifixion and was this a body which He merely assumed to accommodate Himself to the senses of His disciples, not a "real" body at all, and certainly not the same body as He had in His earthly life?

This is a very plausible view to take if the physical seems unreal compared to the spiritual; in which case, the earthly body of Jesus has little or no significance, being simply an instrument, so to speak, to enable Him to carry out His mission on this earth. But this immediately raises the question: "What was His mission?" If, as many people think, including many who call themselves Christians, Jesus was essentially a moral teacher whose role was to give human beings a kind of blueprint of the morality which leads to true human self-fulfillment, then that, in turn, raises the question: "Who was Jesus?" Was He merely a supremely inspired prophet, filled as no one else has ever been with God's Spirit? If so, then His body was not of any great consequence; what mattered was His spiritual genius.

But, of course, that is not what is meant by the Incarnation. What Catholic Christians have always believed is that God, that is, God's very Word or essence, became a human being without ceasing to be God. The humanity the Word assumed was a real, full-blooded human nature; it was not just a disguise, or a prop, or a useful, indeed necessary instrument, to be discarded when it had done its job. The Word of God's humanity, including the body, was not like a wooden leg; it was not artificial, it was a part of Himself, it was integral to Jesus Christ the God-man.

Now, if this is true, then Jesus' physical body, and not only His human soul, is of huge significance. For, as we have seen, Incarnation means that God literally got "under our skin." Not only can human nature never be the same after this salutary invasion, but the actual body that belonged to the Word was like no other body that has ever existed. This body was literally filled with divinity, irradiated by the presence of God. During His earthly life the divinity was kept carefully veiled—with one exception: the occasion on which the Transfiguration took place immediately prior to the arrival of Jesus and His disciples in Jerusalem, ostensibly to celebrate the Jewish Passover, but in reality to institute an altogether new Passover meal before Jesus was executed. For one unique moment, the divinity of Jesus is permitted to stream out, so to speak, to the amazed awe of the disciples. What was normally kept out of sight as too "aweful" a reality for human beings—and inappropriate anyway for display, given that God wanted to join the human race and to share in our human life, not to brandish His divinity before His creatures—was for once allowed to be seen by His intimate circle as a prelude to the shocking events they were about to witness.

But that unique body, unlike any mere human body, could hardly be allowed to molder away in the ground, nor could it just be discarded since it belonged to Jesus, the Son of God. If you think that human beings consist of both the physical and the spiritual, of both body and soul, then human beings cannot be divested of their bodies without ceasing to be the same human beings as they were before. Likewise, Jesus Christ cannot continue to exist without continuing to be the incarnate Word of God, the God-man, which also means that He cannot continue to be properly human without retaining His body. When Jesus appeared to His disciples after clearly dying and told them that these real but mysterious appearances would not be continuing, but that He would be returning to heaven, He didn't imply or indicate that He was reverting to His pre-incarnation state, that the Word or Son of God was now about to discard all semblance of the humanity which He had only temporarily adopted or borrowed in order to accomplish His mission on earth. Naturally, in that case, His human body would cease to have any significance. The corollary of such an announcement would have been that the Resurrection was to be understood by the disciples in a purely spiritual sense. The idea of resurrecting a body that was only an ephemeral instrument would be absurd. Whatever the truth might be about the bodily manifestations reported by the gospel writers, it would certainly not have been of any lasting significance. These manifestations would either not have been intended to be understood by the writers in any literal sense, or they would have been miraculous occurrences but absolutely exceptional in the sense that the disciples would in no way have intended to interpret them as meaning that Jesus' bodily humanity would continue after His return to God the Father.

However, what Jesus actually tells the disciples is that He is going ahead of them as the same Jesus they had known on earth, although of course He was now raised from the dead and enjoying heavenly life. The important thing was that He never hinted in any way at all that the Jesus who was now revealed to them as the God-man would cease to be this Jesus after He had ascended to the Father, that He would no longer be man as well as God, human as well as divine. On the contrary, the Resurrection followed by the Ascension showed that the humanity assumed by the Word of God was forever assumed, forever taken up into the Godhead. Certainly, this humanity was now changed but the identity with the earthly Jesus remained. Jesus' promise was that all the human race could from now on share in His Resurrection and Ascension. He had gone on ahead as the leader. The human race descended from the first man, Adam, now had a new progenitor in the God-man. Or, to put it in another way, Jesus is there in heaven as the elder brother of a new liberated human family, who cannot obviously be the Son of God as He is, but who can become adopted children, can in a very real sense become members of the trinitarian family by virtue of the humanity eternally embraced by the Word.

The implications of the Resurrection, therefore, are momentous—more tremendous than Catholic Christians in the West have sometimes appreciated. In the Byzantine tradition preserved by the Orthodox Church and also Eastern Churches in communion with the Pope, the sense of the potential for the material and the physical to be impregnated, transformed by the spiritual and transcendent, has always been greater. There is not the same sort of rigid separation between the two spheres as has often been assumed in the West. Thus Western or Latin Catholics have statues in their churches, but they don't revere and pray to them as Easterners venerate their icons, through which they feel themselves to be in direct contact with the supernatural. For them, the moment of the Transfiguration is hugely significant because it reveals how what is material can be divinized. The glory of God that shines through the man Jesus is something that continues to shine through His Church: the supernatural has through the Incarnation entered what is earthly and physical.

Nevertheless, this belief in and sense of the way in which the spiritual and supernatural have been irrevocably united with the material, able to impregnate and transform it, is the key to understanding aspects of Catholicism which can be so baffling, not to say repugnant, to outsiders. It explains at the simplest level why Catholic churches contain pictures, statues, and all the other visual and tangible things encountered in them. To be shocked by them is like being shocked by seeing portraits and photographs of family members in a house, or being surprised by the way in which people keep things which belonged to and which they associate with the dead. Somebody very obtuse might question why anyone should need such things—merely physical things—to keep the dead person's memory alive. Surely to love somebody is a matter of the heart and emotions: to hanker after material things to remind one of loved ones, whether alive or dead, is to admit that one's love is not very deep or lasting. For how can what pertains to our psychological and spiritual being be in any way dependent on the physical? We shall be saying more about what is an indisputable fact, whether one likes it or not, later. Even if it does reveal the weakness of the fickle human heart, it still demonstrates that the materialism of Catholicism which strikes so many people as totally unspiritual is no different really from what all human beings do naturally, whatever their religion or lack of religion.

This point is relevant to a practice, which is likely, more than anything else, to affront and repel non-Catholics, and even some Catholics who have been over-spiritualized, as it were, by their environment. The preservation of relics of the saints is only a religious equivalent of what ordinary human beings do without hesitation when it comes to members of their families. And, of course, the saints *are* members of the family of the God-man. To visit the grave of a loved one is a very common and natural thing to do, but what about the preservation of a saint's body on display in a glass case in a Catholic church? Again, this becomes less strange, less repugnant perhaps, when one remembers the importance, the intrinsic value, of the human body from the Christian point of view. Even from a mere human point of view, as we have seen, we cannot imagine a bodiless human being. The body is integral to the human person. As with Jesus, then, if the human person is to live on after death, somehow the body must also live on if it is going to be the same person in any meaningful way that we can understand. Quite apart from that, if human beings have a spiritual component called the soul, then that does not detract from, but rather, enhances that which embodies it. And this leads us to another consideration which we shall have to deal with in the next chapter: the idea that Christians are walking temples, as Saint Paul puts it, or churches containing the Holy Spirit. If that is so, then bodies are not to be sniffed at—and certainly not the bodies of those people we call saints, who have allowed the Holy Spirit truly to divinize their selves, which necessarily includes their bodies.

Finally, to return to the Resurrection itself, the Protestant tendency to rigidly separate the material from the spiritual can be very damaging to a proper understanding of it. It can lead to a false alternative: either the Resurrection must be straightforwardly physical, that is, a resuscitation, or it must be a purely spiritual phenomenon. For liberal Protestants the first alternative is the literal, simple-minded interpretation. But, in fact, as we have seen, it hardly does justice to the accounts in the Gospels, which, understood quite literally, do not actually support this view of the Resurrection. On the other hand, if it was an entirely spiritual happening in the minds of the apostles, then, equally, how do we account for their sheer astonishment which the gospel stories make no effort to conceal and which gives little credit to the faith of the disciples? Certainly, we could imagine Peter suggesting to the others that perhaps if they carried out Jesus' last mandate to them and repeated what He had done at their last meal together, somehow He would be with them again in spirit. Or again, simply, if the scene in the Gospels was that of the apostles fervently praying and full of confidence that their prayers would make Jesus present again to them, then one could explain the Resurrection in exclusively spiritual terms. But, in fact, if we are to put any credence in the Gospels, something absolutely startling and unexpected happened to those disillusioned, frightened apostles, who had refused even to believe the women disciples who were the first witnesses of the Resurrection. It was no figment of their imagination.

CHAPTER 8

WE SEND YOU OUR LOVE

The New Testament tells us that the turning point for the disciples of Jesus in terms of their faith and confidence was not so much the Resurrection as the mysterious event that occurred at the Jewish harvest feast, which took place fifty days—hence its Greek name "Pentecost"—after the Passover feast. That sacred meal had been taken over by Jesus to institute a new meal of remembrance to signal the "passing over" of the whole human race from slavery to sin to freedom as liberated children of God. Now Pentecost was totally eclipsed by the fulfillment of Jesus' promise to His disciples that shortly they would be "baptized with the Holy Spirit." Suddenly a gale seemed to blow through the house where the disciples and Mary, together with other close associates of Jesus, were meeting for the Jewish feast. This was the moment when the new People of God, the Church, are finally instituted as the body in and through which Jesus will continue to live and act. On the night before He died at the Last Supper, Jesus had promised His disciples that when He returned to His Father He would ask Him to send them the Holy Spirit in His name who would lead, support, and teach them.

The Old Testament tells of several theophanies or manifestations of God in which He speaks to His chosen people, most importantly of all on Sinai when He gives His law and commandments to Moses, veiled by a cloud which partially reveals and partially conceals Him. This cloud was understood in the Christian tradition to be an image of the Holy Spirit. Unfortunately, as we have seen, the fact that the Jews had an understanding of God's moral law, which was unique, only worsened their situation insofar as they, in consequence, possessed an especially acute awareness of sin, combined with the helplessness of fallen human beings to resist sin. The expectation of a Messiah was coupled with an anticipation that He would bring a new Spirit to renew the human heart. With hearts no longer made of stone but alive with a new life, human beings would be capable of keeping God's commandments, which would no longer be just external edicts to obey, inevitably alien and foreign to fallen humanity, but now a part of their very fabric. Creation would then be transformed.

On that feast of Pentecost, when the Jews celebrated the life-giving harvest, these anticipations and expectations were seen by Jesus' closest adherents to be fulfilled. Miraculously, tongues of fire appeared to alight on their heads, and at the same time they suddenly found themselves speaking in foreign languages, as though symbolizing a new unity and reconciliation among peoples divided from each other by sin. The man Jesus had appointed as the head apostle, Peter, who had denied he had anything to do with Jesus after His arrest, and who had doubted the story of the women who first reported the Resurrection to the disciples, now, seemingly without hesitation, gets up and publicly announces that the promised Spirit has come, having been received from the Father and then sent to them by the Jesus who had been executed and then raised to new life.

From then on a strange courage and fearlessness seem to possess the disciples. The same disciples who had so often failed to understand when Jesus was with them, who had hidden in terror after His death, who had been amazed and doubtful about the Resurrection right up until the Ascension, now suddenly become filled with daring faith, ready to risk death for Jesus, whom they recognize not just to be the Messiah but God Himself. If we are to give any credence to the New Testament accounts, something very dramatic had clearly affected them. Surely, one might think, the Resurrection itself should have cleared away any doubts they had; surely then they would have realized who Jesus was. But according to the New Testament account, it is only at Pentecost that all doubts disappear. And not only that, but an extraordinary confidence and fearlessness take hold of the apostles, especially Peter, who takes the lead in publicly proclaiming the Resurrection and what it implies about the identity of Jesus. We are left with this paradox, then: that it is neither the earthly nor the risen Jesus who completely and immediately convinces the disciples, putting radically new heart into them. No, it is this mysterious Spirit, like the Messiah long expected by the Jews, who finally and definitely reveals the identity of Jesus. Jesus had told them this Spirit would come, sent by Him from the Father, and would empower them for the mission that lay ahead of them.

Now one might have thought that the disciples would feel tricked by what seemed very intangible compared to the real Jesus, alive or risen. But the curious fact is that Jesus, even when He appeared to them after the Resurrection, did not, in fact, have the effect on them that this Spirit has. And certainly, there is absolutely no hint at all that the disciples felt in any way cheated, or even nostalgic for Jesus. There is never the slightest sense, even on the part of the disciple personally closest to Jesus, that the disciples "missed" Jesus or regretted that He had to go, leaving them some rather shadowy Spirit. Nor again does Jesus Himself indicate that they have to accept that, with His own mission complete, He now wishes naturally to return to His Father, but that, instead, He and His Father will provide a sort of substitute for Him—not the real thing, as it were, but a passable compensation for the loss of Jesus Himself.

No, what Jesus tells them on the night before He dies is that they must wait for the Spirit, who will reveal the whole truth to them and who will "glorify" Him to them. The final act of the great drama of the Incarnation is not going to feature Jesus Himself personally but this Spirit—and yet the Spirit has no other role except to tell them about Jesus. There is no suggestion at all that the Spirit has any job to tell them about the Spirit. This Spirit who is to empower the disciples is only in fact concerned with Jesus. And this is the reason why, of course, the disciples after Pentecost had no regrets, no sense of loss. For what is abundantly clear is that, far from having lost Jesus, Jesus is now actually *more* real, *more* really present to them, than He ever was during His earthly or risen life.

For the Spirit not only reveals the real Jesus to them, but the Spirit actually, mysteriously, makes Jesus present to them. It is as if they now encounter the real Jesus for the first time. Because of this Spirit now within them, they discover that Jesus can now be far more deeply, more intimately, present to them than when they could physically see and touch Him and talk to Him. How could this be?

I think there is a human analogy which can throw light on this. We all know the expressions "familiarity breeds contempt" and "absence makes the heart grow fonder". When somebody is always around, it's easy to take him for granted. It's often when he is not there that he comes more vividly before our mind's eye; certainly we think of him with a renewed appreciation. And when somebody we love has died, it is paradoxical, but probably true, that we feel a surge and strength of love that we never felt before, if only because now we forget or ignore the things that made us impatient with him when he was alive. Death has a wonderful effect of leaving only pleasant memories. It's a simple fact of human life that absence and loss change our perspective: no one is more patriotic than the person who lives abroad.

To try to understand why it was that Pentecost apparently changed the whole attitude of the disciples, we need to realize that with the arrival of the Spirit their appreciation of who this Jesus was, who during His earthly life had been for them essentially a mysterious teacher and healer, suddenly took on a new dimension. And the reason is that the Spirit didn't come to reveal the Spirit to them but to open their eyes fully at last to who Jesus really was. Just as an absent or dead person can somehow strangely be fully appreciated only when he is no longer with us, so, far from the Spirit being a compensation, a poor substitute for Jesus, it was through the Spirit that Jesus, the risen Lord, now becomes fully real to them. Indeed, Jesus becomes intimately present to each of them as He could never have been in His earthly life, or even in His Resurrection appearances. For what the Spirit does is bring the incarnate, the crucified, the risen, the ascended, and the glorified Christ into their very hearts. He is no longer external to them; they experience Him now in the depths of their being. This explains why all the fear vanishes, all doubts evaporate, why they are now consumed with a faith which sadly they could never summon when Jesus was actually with them. How was this?

Another analogy may help. When "Joe" goes away on holiday with his friend "John," "Joe" is quite likely to send a postcard to another friend, ending, "John sends his love, too." Now, the friend who receives the card is not going to be on the look out for the parcel post, expectantly waiting for a package to arrive containing this promised "love." But when Jesus promised His disciples that He would ask the Father for the Holy Spirit to send to them, He really was speaking very literally. For who, after all, is the Holy Spirit? If God is love, then God's Spirit can be nothing other than Love itself. Consequently, one may surely and literally interpret Jesus as saying that He and the Father will send the disciples their Spirit who is Love. As we saw in an earlier chapter, the Holy Spirit is the Love the Father has for His Word or essence, who inevitably has the same love for His Father. And this mutual Love is the Holy Spirit of Love. And so Jesus fulfils His solemn promise by sending, on that fateful day, the Love of God into the disciples' hearts. But unlike the friend's love, which has to remain in His absence a matter of words, this Love which the Father sends via the Son is not, and cannot necessarily be, a mere matter of words. This Love is an active and dynamic Person, not a mere sentiment. Quite literally, Jesus meant, "We shall send you our love," but that Love is not a thing but a person, the Holy Spirit. And so it is this Person who dramatically "invades" the lives of the disciples at Pentecost.

Another very important reason why Jesus was not in any way "tricking" His followers with a poor substitute for Himself is that *He too* required the Holy Spirit for *His* mission and work. In other words, the Pentecost experience of the disciples mirrored Jesus' own experience.

In the Old Testament we see the Spirit, while remaining hidden, revealing God the Father to the Jews. But in the New Testament, the same Spirit now makes known the Word, which (or rather who) is the expression of the Father. Again, the Spirit's job is not to reveal the Spirit, but to unveil Christ. Self-effacingly, the Spirit solely enables the visible image of the invisible God be seen in the fullness of His love by human beings for the first time. Jesus cannot manage on His own. He is distinct but inseparable from, and indeed dependent on, the Spirit. Without the Spirit, Mary, His mother, could never have become pregnant. She conceived, not as a result of sexual intercourse with Joseph, but through spiritual intercourse with the

Spirit, so to speak. The Spirit comes down on her, according to the Gospels, meaning that she is literally penetrated and impregnated by the mutual love of the Father and the Son. In love with God's Love, Mary becomes literally full of God, to whom she then gives birth. But the Spirit's mission doesn't end there. For after all, we must once again remind ourselves who the Spirit is. The Spirit is the Spirit of Jesus' own life, the love He has for His Father and the love the Father has for Him. Jesus Christ, the God-man, can obviously do nothing, cannot be at all, without the Love that is God.

Before beginning His public mission, Jesus asks the last of the Old Testament prophets, John the Baptist, to baptize Him. This baptism that John was trying to get his fellow Jews to accept was a concrete and visible sign. Immersion in water, symbolizing purification and renewal, signifies that they were ready to begin a new life of fidelity to God, indeed confessing their sins to John as he baptized them and actively preparing themselves for the arrival of the long-awaited Messiah, who was now felt to be imminent. When Jesus asks for baptism, John protests. He says that it is *he* who needs baptism at Jesus' hands. But Jesus is insistent and receives a baptism which couldn't actually of itself produce any effect, any more than the law of God to which the Jews had unique access could effect the change of heart and the motivation necessary for fallen human beings to carry out successfully what they knew in their conscience they ought to do.

But this merely symbolic rite is immediately followed by a very mysterious occurrence. Having emerged from the water, according to the gospel account, Jesus now sees what appears to be a dove coming down out of the sky on to Him. It is, in fact, the Holy Spirit coming to consecrate Him as the expected Messiah, about to begin His mission. At the same time, He hears a voice saying, "This is my Son, the loved one." Following this, Jesus, we are told, is then led by the same Spirit to the desert where He undergoes the ordeal of the devil's temptations. This is part of being human, so Jesus had to undergo this experience. We need to remember, of course, that these "temptations" were no more tempting to Jesus than the "temptation" to mug old ladies or to put people in gas chambers tempts most of us. There could be no struggle for Jesus; it was simply a matter of repelling these suggestions from the devil. Jesus' humanity was fully human without any trace of inhumanity. The impossibility of His being "tempted" by choices less than good does indeed set Him apart from the rest of us, but the possibility of being in any way inhuman was not and could not be part of the Incarnation. The nearest that Jesus could get to sin, not only as the Word of God but as the most human of human beings, was at His execution when He finally accepted what had to be the most terrible of all sufferings for Him, that of experiencing the dreadful alienation from God that is the consequence of sin, but the actual experience of sinning was incompatible with both His divine *and* His human nature.

Having decisively repudiated the idea of being a political messiah with temporal powers and privileges, Jesus begins His mission by going into the synagogue at Nazareth on the Jewish Sabbath and reading out a famous passage from the prophet Isaiah about the advent of the Spirit, which He clearly applies to Himself. From this inauguration onward, Jesus' mission is a joint one with the Spirit. Frequently alluding to the Spirit in His teaching, He at last promises, on the night before He dies, that this Spirit who has been with Him during His earthly life and mission will also be given to His disciples. And when He rose from the dead, that's exactly what happened when He said to the disciples, "Receive the Holy Spirit." Immediately prior to this, He had announced to them, "As the Father sent me, so am I sending you." In other words, the joint mission of Jesus and the Spirit is now to be handed over to the Church. And so, on Pentecost the fullness of the Spirit is finally given to the Church.

The corollary of this is that the Trinity is now also fully revealed. By receiving the Spirit in the Church, human beings are now privileged to have a share in the community of the three Persons, to participate in the life of the Godhead. Humans made in the image of God can now actually enjoy not just intimate friendship with God but a part in the life of the Trinity. In spite of the Fall, God's ultimate plan in creating us comes to fruition. The creatures He had made to be like Him, as far as possible, are now entitled, as it were, to come up to the top table. By God's Word coming down to our level, we can be drawn up to His level. Without actually becoming God, thanks to Jesus Christ, we are now in a position to become godlike. Again, this is possible only because God's Spirit has entered us. We can be temples, as Saint Paul puts it, or churches, as we might say, of the Holy Spirit. We carry God around within us. By coming not just close to us, but actually within us, God's Spirit enables or empowers us to enter into His divine life. Saint Paul's analogy is that of adopted children. An adopted child is not literally and biologically the child of its foster parents, but is treated as such. It is a very daring parallel to show just how high the Incarnation, the Resurrection, and finally the coming of the Holy Spirit, have raised even fallen human beings. In spite of all the surrounding polytheism, the Fathers did not hesitate to say that this put us in the position of gods. Or rather, human beings now had the possibility to be gods, truly godlike. Unfortunately only a comparatively few people have manifestly achieved this potential. These men and women are called "saints" and are perhaps the best and most tangible argument for the truth of Catholic Christianity

The world in fact recognizes that there is something special about someone like Mother Teresa of Calcutta. What is this special quality? It surely isn't that she happened only to be more virtuous, more self-controlled, more idealistic than the run of humanity. There are many beliefs and ideologies in the world which encourage and help people to be good, to care about other human beings, often in the most self-sacrificing way. Yet do they, in fact, produce people like Mother Teresa, Saint Francis of Assisi, and all those others the Catholic Church recognizes as saints? It is impossible to prove something like this in the ordinary sense of the word "prove." It would not, after all, be so surprising if these so-called saints believed something—however misguidedly—which nobody else does believe. Even a totally illusory belief could conceivably give people an impetus which they could not get from anywhere else.

For we are not really talking just about goodness or virtue; we are, in fact, talking about something really rather different. We are talking about this so-called Holy Spirit. We are talking about the God who is Love actually sending this Love into human hearts. We are not talking just about God telling us He loves us, or even sending us some sign or token of His love. If God in fact gives us His Holy Spirit, penetrates us with His Holy Spirit, then God is transmitting to us the Love which is His life. This is the fulfillment of the famous prophecy in the Old Testament when God announces to His chosen people: "I will sprinkle clean water upon you, and you shall be clean from all your uncleannesses, and from all your idols I will cleanse you. A new heart I will give you, and a new spirit I will put within you; and I will take out of your flesh the heart of stone and give you a heart of flesh. And I will put my spirit within you" (Ezekiel 36:25-27a). It is as if God is promising His people a kind of spiritual transplant, whereby He will engraft His heart or spirit into His people. When a transplant takes place in an operation, an organ from somebody else's body is implanted into the body of the sick person. So, in effect, what we have here is an extraordinary promise that human beings, wounded by and suffering from sin, are going to be donated something that belongs to their Creator. God, as donor, will arrange for the transplant of His spirit into us. Of course, this spirit must, in fact, be His Holy Spirit.

For human beings to be able to really be like their Maker, that is to say, to be able to love as God loves, since God is Love, we need not just God's help. The Jews had that aid above all in the form of the revelation of God's commandments. As we have seen, that was not enough. Knowing but being unable to act on what they knew made their plight even more wretched in one way than that of their unenlightened pagan neighbors. In order to love as God loves, fallen human beings needed the equivalent of a transplant, that is, a new heart able to beat with God's love. It is this Love which is the life of the Trinity that is given to human beings, who now become empowered even to dare to call God their "Father." The transcendent God of Judaism could not be directly referred to by His name, "Yahweh," for fear of implying lack of reverence. When, then, Jesus tells His followers that they must pray to God as their "Father," He is saying something quite revolutionary. He is overturning their whole idea of God, so infinitely above humans that He may not even be referred to by name. Now He may actually be addressed as the Father of His family.

CHAPTER 9

WHY THE CHURCH?

We have seen how it appears that the arrival of the Spirit at Pentecost empowered the disciples with the presence and strength of Jesus Christ in a way in which they had never been before. The fact that Jesus could now be more intimately available, as it were, also meant that His availability was no longer restricted as before. During His earthly life, He had been subject, like other human beings, to the ordinary restrictions of space and time. Even during the Resurrection appearances when these restrictions no longer applied in the same way, He still could not live in the hearts of human beings, countless human beings, as He could from the time of Pentecost.

From then on, Jesus could be immediately present wherever the Spirit was present.

From then on, the joint mission of Christ and the Holy Spirit becomes the joint mission of the Church and the Spirit. For what, after all, is the Church but the place where the Spirit is to be found? The Spirit takes possession of the individual Christian, but since it is the same Spirit in everyone, all those who are occupied by the Spirit are also united by their common possession of the Spirit. Of course, they are also united at the same time by having Christ immediately and intimately present to them through the Spirit whose business is not to manifest the Spirit but Christ, and indeed the Father also, since where the mutual love of Father and Son is present, that is, the Spirit, there too must be present the Father and the Son. Apart from that, anyway, the Christ, who is now with His Father in heaven but who is also within those occupied by the Spirit, creates a new unity between the Creator and His creatures. The spiritual unity that exists between all those possessed of the Spirit is essentially what is meant by the Church. Just as each member of the Church is said by Saint Paul to be a "temple" of the Holy Spirit, so too the whole Church is the "temple" of the Holy Spirit. Since each member of the Church also possesses Christ by virtue of the Spirit, the Church is also called by Saint Paul "the Body of Christ." This is also, of course, true in an even more concrete way since the members of the Church share in what Saint Paul calls "the one loaf" and "the one cup" of the new Passover meal, the Eucharist.

The mission of Christ and the Holy Spirit is, then, continued by the Church which is both "the body of Christ" and "the temple of the Holy Spirit." This concept of the supernatural nature of the Church is what lies at the heart of Catholicism. It explains why the Creed professes belief in the *oneness* of the Church as an article of faith. The Catholic belief is not that the Church is "one" simply by virtue of the fact that all Christians profess some sort of belief in Christ; nor is it just an aspiration or ideal, as if oneness were something desirable because it would be convenient and organizationally useful if all Christians were in the same Church. No, the Catholic belief is that just as there is only one baptism, so there is only one Church into which it is possible to be baptized. What happens afterward to the baptized person is another matter, but to begin with, everyone belongs to only one Church. It doesn't matter whether you are an Anglican or an Orthodox or a Methodist; at your baptism, according to Catholic theology, you became a member of the Catholic Church. This is the basis of Catholic ecumenism which recognizes this basic, underlying unity of all baptized Christians, even though this unity is later broken, through no fault of those who have simply inherited the disunity caused by their ancestors. While this recognition of membership through baptism establishes at least a partial oneness or communion, the Catholic understanding of the nature of the Church means that *full* membership in the Church is restricted to Catholics.

For whereas Protestants may think that the oneness already achieved by baptism is all that the Creed means—and that any more visible unity is a more or less desirable goal—for Catholics a visible unity is rather of the essence of the Church as Jesus intended it to be. After all, the original chosen people consisted of one people, the Jewish people. The new chosen people of Christ were no longer limited to the Jews but they were still intended to have a unity, although no longer a racial unity. The whole point of the mission of the Incarnate Word of God and the Holy Spirit was not only to reconcile fallen human beings with their Creator God but, also, to restore unity *among* human beings who were alienated from each other through sin, as well as from God. This unity is to be achieved through making human beings one in the unity of the Body of Christ, the Church. Possession of a common baptism by itself would not be enough. Just as the Jewish people were recognizably and visibly the Jewish people, so, too, the new People of God must also be manifestly one. The unity of baptism by itself is not enough. Above all, there must be oneness at the meal commemorating the new Passover. The new People of God must both signify and actually bring about unity among human beings separated from each other by sin, as well as unity or communion with God. Or rather, it is the latter which makes possible a new unity for humankind. And this unity is meant to reflect the divine model, the unity in love of the three Persons of the Trinity.

Actually, of course, this reuniting of God with human beings and of human beings among themselves must be a simultaneous process. To have imperfect union with God is to have imperfect union with other human beings, and vice versa. We get back into a close relationship with God by sharing in His divine life, but this cannot happen fully except in one Church where human beings are fully in union with each other. The oneness of the Church, therefore, is a necessity not an option. If baptism were all that were essential for full membership in the Church, then this would not perhaps be so. We have to make sense of not only what Jesus did on the night before He died, but, also, take into account the quite extraordinary powers which, according to the Gospel, He gave His disciples. Thus He told the apostles that He was giving them the authority to forgive sins, a prerogative that for the Jews was reserved to God; indeed, it was Jesus' own claim to be able to do this that was a chief part of their charge against Him of blasphemy. He gave them a solemn mandate to teach in His name saying that their voice would be His voice; He promised them that the Holy Spirit would "guide [them] into all the truth" (John 16:13).

Now, of course, it is quite possible to argue that these powers were only intended for the apostles in order to get Christianity going in the world. There are problems, however, about this line of argument. After all, apparently without any specific instructions, the remaining eleven apostles, following the treachery and suicide of Judas, did not hesitate to appoint a successor to him. Already, even before the decisive moment of Pentecost, they knew that they must fill the vacancy with one of the disciples who had been a witness to all the crucial events. Thus, right from the beginning it is readily understood that Jesus' arrangements for His Church were intended to last, as well as, presumably, the original powers He gave the apostles. It was not a temporary state of affairs intended just for the original foundation. No, the evidence of the New Testament and the first age of the Church show a continuity, as well as a confidence, to develop. For example, with the death of the first generation and the rapid growth of the Church, we find that the twelve apostles, clearly signifying for the Jews the twelve tribes of Israel, are succeeded by leaders called *episcopoi* in Greek, the language of the New Testament and the early Church, or "bishops" in English.

Even if we didn't have the historical record to show that Jesus' intentions for His Church persisted, albeit in adapted forms, we would surely expect this to be the case. If the mission of Jesus was intended to outlast that first generation—as it presumably was or, otherwise, there was not much point in it at all—then what He instituted was intended to be permanent. For example, His solemn instruction to the apostles at the Last Supper to do what He had done has always been understood by Christians through the centuries to be a lasting mandate, whatever their understanding of that event has been.

It was only in the sixteenth century at the Reformation that really sizeable numbers of Christians begin to entertain a much "lower" view of the Church, although they differed among themselves. It was only in the sixteenth century that people begin to seriously appeal to the Bible against Church teaching, as though the Church was subordinate to Scripture. Of course, reformers had constantly invoked the Scriptures to correct abuses in the Church, but that was very different from actually setting them against the Catholic Church to correct alleged incorrect teachings. In other words, it becomes possible, indeed normal, to believe that the Church can fall into serious error, in spite of Jesus' promise of the Holy Spirit. This is the most significant aspect of the Reformation. Certainly, the so-called Reformers, all of whom had naturally been members of the Catholic Church before breaking away to form their own denominations, differed greatly among themselves as to what the Bible actually did say. Where they were in agreement was in the belief that in principle it is possible, even desirable, to separate the Scriptures from the Church and to believe that the successors of the original apostles might not only have failed to live up to the spirit of Scripture, to the moral teachings of Christ, but actually to have led the Church into serious error on matters of doctrine.

The fact is that the most fundamental difference between Catholics and Protestants is not always understood. Many people suppose that Catholicism is simply Bible Christianity, that is, Protestantism, plus a whole lot of accretions, some bad, some indifferent, some perhaps acceptable but not necessary. The truth is that the two religions are essentially different in kind, because they have diametrically opposed views of the relation of the Church to the Christian faith, as well as to the Bible. The crucial and fundamental difference between Catholic and Protestant understanding of the nature of the Church is that Protestants think of the Christian faith as existing somehow independently of the Church, whereas, for Catholics, you cannot separate the two from each other. For many Protestants, the Christian faith is something you find in the Bible, and you then look around for the church which seems most in conformity with this. But for Catholics, the Bible is the possession of the Church, which is entrusted with interpreting it. They point to the fact that it was the Church, which called itself Catholic, that decided in the early centuries what books of the Old Testament and which writings relating to Jesus Christ were to be included as authentic parts of Scripture. After all, the books of the Old Testament were originally the self-expression of the first chosen People of God, and those of the New Testament were that of the Church of the apostles.

But quite apart from that, Catholics also point out that the first preaching of the Gospel was done before any of the New Testament writings were even available—for they were written by that Church of the New Testament. In other words, it was the Church which began at Pentecost to announce the news about the risen Jesus and that there was now a new People of God which one had to join by baptism in order to be a follower of Jesus. This same Church also took upon itself, as Jesus Himself had done, to interpret the Old Testament in the light of God's self-revelation in Jesus. Obviously, the Church at the beginning could not even appeal to the New Testament because it had not yet been written.

Scripture is not in the forefront, with the Church standing in the background. For Catholics, it is the Church which teaches the faith, always necessarily in accordance with the Word of God contained in Scripture, the unique and definitive account of God's unfolding revelation of Himself. A book like the Bible obviously cannot speak for itself. It has to be read and it has to be interpreted. In actual practice, the vast majority of Christians interpret it in the light of the particular church and tradition in which they have been brought up. But the large number of Protestant churches show how many differing interpretations and understandings are possible—as must be the case with any book. And so, while it could be very misleading to say that the Church is more *important* than the Bible, the Catholic position is that the Church is prior to the Bible—the chosen Jewish people to the Old Testament and the Christian Church to the New Testament.

As we have already noticed, had Jesus told the apostles that they should write down a record of what they had heard and seen, which would constitute the definitive guide for all their teaching, we should expect the gospel writers to mention this very explicitly as their authorization for writing the Gospel. Instead, what we find is Jesus expressly authorizing *them* to be His representatives and the communicators of His revelation. And not only that, He also places one of them at the head—not the disciple who was closest to Him personally but the disciple who gave as nearly the right answer as he could when Jesus asked them who He was. This apostle, called Simon, He now re-names "Rock," "Peter" in the original Greek of the New Testament. Peter's faith is to be the "rock" on which Jesus intends to build His Church. It was this that made Peter's cowardly failure all the more shocking. Three times he denied, on being challenged after Jesus' arrest, that he was one of His associates.

Now, just as Jesus could hardly have intended the first apostles not to be replaced, or the new Passover meal to cease to be celebrated after their deaths, so His appointment of one of the apostles to be the senior one was presumably meant to be of a permanent nature and not merely limited to Simon Peter. Of course, when one thinks about it, the Church would surely have had to invent a Peter if Jesus had not already done so. For if the Church was really intended to be truly *one*, not simply in some vague spiritual sense but in a visible and concrete form corresponding to an actual human community or society, then there had to be somebody at the head. After all, every nation has to have a head of state, and this new People of God could not be left to the apostles and their successors to run without some kind of a structure of leadership. What if the apostles disagreed among themselves? There had to be one who was recognized as the leader, as in any group. This presupposes that Jesus had in mind a People of God as clearly one as the Jewish people were one racially. If, on the other hand, one thinks of the Christian Church as a kind of abstraction meaning really all the independent churches that claim to be Christian, then no doubt no leader is necessary, any more than a large extended family requires somebody at the head to survive. It might be convenient from a practical point of view on important family occasions that the different branches should acknowledge one person as the patriarch or matriarch. But the lack of such a person doesn't in any way affect the status of all the branches of that extended family as being truly members of the family, all descended from common ancestors. It is obvious, however, that such a family is not really one as the members of an immediate family who live under one roof are one. They may get together on important occasions, but in practice they live their lives apart, perhaps very far apart, both geographically and in other ways. There are resemblances, ties in common, but otherwise perhaps very little indeed to make them want to live together in one community.

That, in fact, is very much the situation of many of those who call themselves Christians. They differ widely among themselves on matters of doctrine and on how they regard Scripture. But, as I have suggested, the crucial convergence between them is the way in which they see the Church. Yes, there is general agreement that Christianity is not meant to be an individualistic, "do-it-yourself" religion. They concur in thinking that Christians will naturally and properly want to come together for worship and to form communities called churches. This word comes from a Greek word meaning "what belongs to the Lord," but the original Greek and Latin words used to describe both the chosen Jewish people coming together for worship and the Christian community mean "assembly." While there may not be any disagreement that Christians should come together in community, by no means do all believe that all Christians should belong to one united assembly or Church. No doubt many would see this as something inherently undesirable. After all, people differ widely in their cultural and other attitudes. Why should they not therefore belong to different groupings—albeit all sharing a common understanding of the Christian faith? What suits Italians may not suit English people—so what is unnatural about the English having their own national church? Others may take a rather different line, arguing that while no doubt a united church would be very desirable in theory, in practice it is an impossible ideal, and that to try and achieve it may do more harm than good.

The Roman Catholic and Orthodox Churches, which were one Church, called the Catholic or universal Church, until the eleventh century when a tragic split occurred more for political than doctrinal differences (which hardly exist), both see the oneness of the Church as an essential mark or note of the Church. The Protestant Churches, which owe their origin to the Reformation of the sixteenth century, see the matter in a very different light. For them, the focus of spiritual (as opposed to any concrete or visible) unity is the Bible. Modern liberal Protestants may take the line that there is no one objective or true interpretation of the Scriptures—each generation and culture understanding the inspired word according to its own best lights. Fundamentalist Protestants reject this approach, insisting that there is no such ambiguity but that the Bible teaches the Christian faith unambiguously. The question of church is very secondary to both groups of Protestants, just as they concur that one belongs to a church where this faith is upheld simply as a matter of convenience and practicality.

This approach is not only quite inconsistent with the internal evidence of the Old and New Testaments, where manifestly the "assembly" of God's people precedes the writing of the Scriptures, which are then authenticated and interpreted by the community. There are also other problems. The very idea that Christianity is what an individual gleans from the Bible effectively rules out the possibility of unity. In other words, Jesus' recorded prayer on the night before He died, that His followers should be one, can only be understood as a pious and, in reality, totally pointless prayer. For we know now, more clearly than people in previous ages, that what a book appears to say depends hugely on the assumptions and perspective of the reader. There is no such thing as a pure meaning which should be transparent to any reader of good will. This does not present the same difficulties for Catholics, as they freely acknowledge, indeed insist, that no book can speak for itself, least of all the book called the Bible which contains so many very heterogeneous writings within itself. No, it obviously needs interpreting, above all by the Spirit-led community in which it was composed and for which it was written. The Jews had the prophets to recall to them the true nature of the covenant and revelation, and the last of them, John the Baptist, paved the way for their fulfillment in Jesus and the new People of God. Without such an authoritative interpretation there will be, or could be, as many different churches as there are different readings. And indeed, the sixteenth-century revolution which detached the Bible from the Church and transferred the teaching authority of the Church to documents which cannot speak for themselves, has certainly led to the formation of many Protestant groups, some, like the Church of England, based on the principle of nationality, others on more of a confessional basis. The Reformation slogan "Scripture alone" was guaranteed in actuality to prevent that unity which Jesus had willed for His Church and which we see in action in the Church of the New Testament, where, whatever the disagreements, it is taken for granted that all the different communities of Christians are bound together in one Gospel which they derive from the teachings of the apostles. In this earliest time of the Church there is no suggestion of a kind of basic Gospel which the apostles in their own different ways broadcast abroad and which they are free to interpret in their own ways and to establish their own various communities. Indeed, in one of his letters Saint Paul delivers a very sharp rebuke to people who claim to be following some particular apostle or teacher, as though the Gospel bore distinctly separate variations which were a matter of choice for the individual (see 1 Cor. 3).

This takes us on to another consideration which the Protestant Reformation fostered: the idea that there is a sort of fundamental Christian faith that is all that really counts and that anything else is more or less optional. This is the idea that there is such a thing as "mere Christianity," to use the term made famous by C. S. Lewis's book. It is an attractive idea, if only because it suggests that whatever differences there may be among Christians, these really pale into insignificance compared to the essential unity which all share by believing in the same fundamental or "mere" Christianity.

Nevertheless, obvious objections spring to mind. In the first place, if the oneness of the Church is something that Jesus intended to be an absolutely essential, not optional, mark of His Church, then mere unity in a common belief would still mean an invisible, spiritual rather than concrete, tangible unity within one community. Or is it suggested that Christians should simply agree to differ on the non-essentials—that is to say, those beliefs which do not belong to the core of belief which is this "fundamental" or "mere" Christianity—and join together on the basis of the most important faith elements which they have in common? Well, it is clear that such a Church would not enjoy a very harmonious unity if there was a widespread disunity, even if only over "less essential" beliefs. But even if one could accept such an imperfect oneness as being all that Jesus really demanded, that still doesn't answer the question: how do we decide what is this "mere" Christianity? And who decides?

Serious differences will come immediately to the fore. Do we decide from the Bible alone? Or from Christian Tradition as well? Or do we agree to treat the past as being all very well for the past—not necessarily binding on us, who have new insights, new knowledge, new problems? However, even if we could all, or most of us, agree on an absolute core of absolutely non-negotiable articles of faith, wouldn't there still be serious problems about other beliefs? What if some people said that certain beliefs, which they had been prepared, in the interests of unity, to exclude from the most important doctrines of all, were still very important to them? And what if others retorted that, far from being important to them, these beliefs were positively distracting from, and therefore damaging to, the core beliefs? Or worse, that they were simply untrue and incompatible with the agreed core beliefs. We should not be surprised that, in fact, there has never existed such a Church of "mere" Christianity.

In response, it could be objected that, while it is true that so far the divisions that began in the sixteenth century have not been solved by means of an agreement on the fundamentals, these are early days, in the sense that the movement for Christian unity has only comparatively recently begun. Or again, the Church of the New Testament could be held up for us as a model. But is there any evidence from the writings that each apostle agreed upon a certain common statement of faith, but also each with his own particular version of it, so that different Christian communities in the different cities of the Roman empire held a variety of different beliefs in addition to the core beliefs?

It is true that on a famous occasion Paul rebuked Peter for giving in to some Jewish converts and appearing by his behavior to imply that the only true Christians were Jews who still practiced Jewish cultic observances. For the first really important doctrinal decision that the early apostolic Church had to face was whether non-Jewish converts had to be circumcised like Jews. And it was Peter, the senior apostle, who took the lead in declaring that it was not necessary, for it had already been revealed to him by God that it was not necessary to adopt the Jewish law in order to become a Christian. Paul's reproach was not against a doctrine that Peter was teaching but against his cowardly and inconsistent behavior. There is absolutely no suggestion in the extent literary records that different apostles taught different variations of the Gospel, with a central core in common. Rather, in his letters to the different "churches" in Corinth, Ephesus, Rome, and so on, Saint Paul stresses the oneness of the Church as the Body of Christ which shares the same faith that comes from himself and the other apostles, the same baptism, and the same Eucharist. Any dissensions or differences that threatened this unity are of the utmost concern to him. And it is quite clear that, for Paul, the unity that existed was not just a happy and convenient fact, which it would be a pity to damage or spoil, but an absolute

CHAPTER 10

THE TWO-FACED CHURCH

If one asks when this Church actually began to exist, one would have to say there were several stages. First of all, Jesus' announcement of the arrival of God's reign on earth marks the inauguration of the Church. Then there is His appointment of the twelve apostles with Peter as their head. The next crucial step is the institution of the new Passover meal, the Eucharist, at the Last Supper: eating Jesus' "body" and drinking His "blood" will be the key way of exercising one's membership in His "Body," the Church. This giving of Himself as the food of the new Passover meal anticipates Jesus' ultimate self-sacrifice on the Cross. This leads on to the next stage. According to one of the Gospels (John 19:31-34), the Roman soldiers, at the request of the Jews who wanted the execution completed before the Saturday which was a Sabbath of special importance, arrived to break the legs of Jesus and His two fellow victims in order to hasten their slow-lingering death. They found that Jesus was already—prematurely, as we have seen—dead. Cheated of this final act of execution, one of the soldiers instead pierced Jesus' side with his lance. The gospel writer then mysteriously adds that blood and water immediately poured out. This strange phenomenon would have struck those first Jewish Christians with its obvious symbolism: the blood symbolizing that of the sacrificial lamb of the Passover meal, and the water, the Spirit that had been promised and prophesied in the Old Testament and alluded to by Jesus Himself, using the same image. The Church Fathers naturally interpreted the water and wine as symbols of Baptism and the Eucharist, the two sacraments signifying the Church which is born like a second Eve from the new Adam. The final step, as we have seen, is Pentecost when the Spirit is sent to the Church, which can now be openly proclaimed.

Now, if we look at these several stages, we can distinguish two different dimensions. On the one hand, there are very concrete and visible elements; on the other hand, there is a more hidden, spiritual aspect. It is the fact that the Church includes both these dimensions which accounts for a good deal of the incomprehension that Catholicism arouses. Thus, for instance, a Protestant may wonder why the Catholic Church is so insistent on the paramount importance of baptizing in water and of using bread and wine at all the main Sunday services. Baptism is, no doubt, mandated in the Gospels and is a useful sign, but surely what is far more important is conversion and faith. Similarly, Jesus certainly instituted an act of worship at the Last Supper involving bread and wine. Does that mean that that has to be the invariable service? Surely other services can also be very important, perhaps even more meaningful and "spiritual" for people— even if a communion service will, like Baptism, always be a useful sign of commitment and badge of membership. Or again, the hierarchical aspect of Catholicism with its stress on pope and bishops will strike many people as more earthly and mundane than heavenly and spiritual. Why do ordinary human beings have to be so significant?

Now the interesting thing is that the Catholic Church also arouses an altogether opposite reaction. For example, it is a source of great puzzlement, even scandal, that it seems to place such value on men and women who separate themselves from the world to devote their days to prayer, when they could be usefully doing good or preaching the Gospel. Outsiders are also conscious that, in spite of all the hierarchical structures of the Church, Catholicism is in other ways less clerical than Protestantism. Some of its members seem as, or more, important than the clergy; people, like Mother Teresa, who after their deaths, may have statues actually erected to them in Catholic churches with people lighting candles and asking for their prayers. In other words, the men and women whom the Catholic Church canonizes as saints seem to be at least as important, if not more important than popes, not to mention bishops and priests. Some of these saints started or inspired religious communities and orders, which also seem to exert great influence in the Catholic Church. Indeed, an attentive observer might conclude that, compared to Protestant churches, the actual bishops and clergy who run the dioceses and parishes are in some ways a good deal less significant than their counterparts among the Protestants. For all its rigidity, formal order, and structure, the Catholic Church seems strangely tolerant, not to say encouraging, of all sorts of people, like Francis of Assisi, with all kinds of different gifts, whom the official authorities of the time may regard as eccentric or worse, and yet who end up by being honored by the Church long after the names of their critics or persecutors, often in very high places, have been forgotten.

What is the explanation for this curious paradox that a Church which lays such huge stress on form and structure should also apparently be so hospitable to another, less external, more spiritual dimension? The answer lies in the two-fold nature of the Church. First and foremost, it must always be emphasized that the Church exists, functions, and lives only in and through the Spirit. Just as Jesus in His earthly life depended totally on the Spirit and yet was a physical, visible human being, so too the Church is not just some invisible spiritual reality, but a highly concrete phenomenon in the world. After all, it consists of human beings, not spirits, although it is only by virtue of the Holy Spirit that the human beings who constitute the Church become and continue to be members of the Church. The Church, then, is both human and divine, visible and spiritual, concrete and hidden. Or to use more theological terms, the Church is at once both hierarchical and mystical.

Because of these two very different aspects of herself, the Catholic Church is a complex and composite reality. This accounts for a good deal of the sheer bewilderment, not to say hostility, that she arouses in those outside her. How can they make any sense of a Church which from one point of view may mean the Vatican, which is not only the center of authority within the Church, but an actual political entity or state, and from a diametrically opposite perspective may mean a cloistered community of nuns, cut off from the outside world, and existing only for purposes of prayer? How can one hope to understand a Church which is at one and the same time a major player on the international stage and yet also claims to be the Church of the poor, one of whose most celebrated members in recent history was a woman who devoted her life to the poorest of the poor? Outsiders are struck by the paradox of a Church which is simultaneously the most worldly of religions and the most spiritual. Even its earthly head, the pope, is called both "Holy Father" and addressed as a sovereign head of state. It is indeed all very puzzling not only for observers but also sometimes for her own members.

But really the "scandal" of the "two-faced" appearance of the Roman Catholic Church can be compared with and traced back to Jesus Christ Himself, that is to say, the "scandal" of the Incarnation itself. It was indeed a scandal to the Jews that an ordinary, however unusual, man should claim, or be claimed by His followers, to be the Son of God. The monotheism which was the boast and unique possession of the Jews could not tolerate the idea that the transcendent Yahweh, who could not even be mentioned by name, should be somehow present in the form of a Jew like themselves. Could this be God Himself, with an actual human mother who was known by name (whoever the father might be—there is internal evidence in the Gospels that there was some doubt about this), who seemed to live like an ordinary human being, but who spoke publicly in an ostensibly unorthodox way, and who was on social terms with immoral and disreputable people on the margins of Jewish society? It was incredible enough, indeed blasphemous, to suggest that God had taken on human form, but the other known facts about Jesus only added insult to injury. And from the point view of a non-Jew, such as a Greek intellectual, the idea that the "Absolute" or the "Word" of Saint John's Gospel (John uses the Greek word "Logos," a word which is most inadequately translated by the English word "Word," since "logos" means not only the word or outward form in which an inward thought is expressed but also the inward thought itself) should become a mere human being was not blasphemous but laughable and unbelievable. For both Jew and Greek the idea that the infinite could become finite in a particular place and a particular time was too shocking or absurd to contemplate.

The Christian claim, then, that this Jew called Jesus was the Son of God was a source of deep scandal to both the most religious and the most philosophical of His contemporaries. The historicity of

Christianity, its belief in the infinite intersecting with the finite, is a continual problem to unbelievers. It is much easier for the human mind—or at least, Christians would say, the fallen human mind—to comprehend absolute perfection or the divine or the One, than to envision the possibility of the explanation and origin of the universe not only coming into the world but actually becoming a part of the world, even becoming a member of the human race, indeed a member of a real human family with a family tree. There is something, even a Christian must admit, just a little beyond belief, beyond the realms of the possible in all this.

This tremendous discrepancy—if the word is appropriate!—between the historical figure, Jesus of Nazareth, and the Son or Word of God, indicates a kind of parallel with the Church which is His Body, and which has both a human and a divine dimension. Of course, the analogy breaks down if only because the contrast between the Church as Holy and the Church as the community of sinful human beings cannot apply to Jesus Christ, who is perfectly human, that is, perfect as God created human beings to be. The Catholic view is that the Church is *really* holy, not just in a pious way of speaking because the Church is the institution which propagates the good news about Jesus—but as being the Body of Christ, the "residence" of the Holy Spirit. No amount of sin on the part of the human beings who belong to it can change that. But the contrast remains glaring. This is another stumbling block for those who are not Catholics. The extraordinarily "high" Catholic concept of the Church seems to them to sit very uncomfortably indeed with the actual failures of Catholics, especially those in positions of authority, to live up to what the Church claims to be.

But quite apart from imperfection and sin, the Church does, like Jesus Christ, have the two sides to her, the human and the divine, and this is always going to be a source of tension within the Church and potential scandal or at least bewilderment to those outside. Because the Church is meant by her founder to be as visible and concrete and tangible as He and the disciples were, and because the oneness of the Church is not a negotiable option but one of the essential properties of the Church, the Church has to have definite, identifiable structures which will maintain her as both visible and one.

Again we must remember that this oneness is not for organizational reasons or for the kind of reasons that the United Nations was set up to bring the nations together into harmonious coexistence. No, the Church *must* be one if she is to be the Church, since she is meant to be the fulfillment of God's plan to restore unity to His creation, a unity which is centered on Christ. Saint Paul dares to liken this unity to marriage, with all its implications of total intimacy and sharing. This communion of love is intended to reflect the communion of the Trinitarian God who is Love. This spiritual dimension of love determines everything else about the Church including its hierarchical character. In this sense Saint John the "beloved" disciple, who was closest to Jesus, is more "important" than Saint Peter who represents authority in the Church. What the person of John represents, love, takes precedence over what the person of Peter represents, because the sole justification for hierarchy is love itself. The appointment of Peter and the other apostles to head the Church is intended by Jesus primarily to maintain the Church as a community of union with God and of union between human beings, a unity which depends on the first unity.

There is another point that should be made here. A "low" view of the Church is bound up with the idea that God saves people through Jesus Christ individually. Just as, for Protestants, the Bible and the Christian faith take precedence over the Church, so is salvation similarly seen as essentially separate from the Church. Certainly, individuals will come into contact with the Jesus of the Bible through an actual Christian community, but the community is in no way integral to the individual's salvation. In other words, you can be saved quite apart from any church. Of course, somebody who has "found" Jesus and has come to believe in Him as the savior will no doubt want eventually to be baptized in some church since the Bible says that that is a necessary token of being a Christian. But on this view, as we shall see, baptism doesn't actually "do" anything to that person. It merely signifies the faith of that person—and a natural desire to share his faith with other Christians in a congenial community. In short, salvation is essentially a purely personal matter, regardless of whatever actual help is given on the way by other Christians and their communities or churches.

Again, this is a fundamental difference between Protestants and Catholics, a difference which precedes any difference in understanding the nature of baptism. There is no point in arguing about the nature of baptism if your real difference is about the nature of salvation itself. For Catholics salvation is not at all a fundamentally personal, in the sense of individualistic, business. On the contrary, the Catholic view is that you cannot get away from the Church: to be saved means joining Christ's Body which is the Church. You simply cannot be a freelance, do-it-yourself, Christian. True, each person is a unique individual, not just a unit in a collective mass, with a unique personal relationship with God, but each individual is also a member of the human race in an inescapable, social relationship with other human beings. To be saved by Christ is to become incorporated in that new community of love and unity which is His Church. That doesn't mean that God has no other way of saving people—God can do anything. But it does mean that this is the way Jesus commanded, and therefore the way God wants—for the very good reason that salvation *means* being restored into unity with God and your fellow human beings. A totally individualistic salvation could not be a proper salvation at all, for salvation means, simultaneously, reconciliation with God *and* with other human beings.

An analogy may help to explain why the Church has to be an integral part of salvation. Suppose a Jew was trying to escape from Nazi persecution in Germany. He might successfully manage to cross the frontier into, say, Switzerland, but without an entry visa he could be subject to return to Germany. For a Jewish refugee to be saved, it was not enough to escape from Germany; there was still the problem of where to go. Freedom from persecution involves not only escaping, but also having a refuge. It is impossible for anyone to live in a void. Life at every level demands a community or society in which to live. In a similar sort of way, the person who believes that Jesus died on the cross to save him is certainly on his way to salvation and has taken the first necessary step to escape from the imprisonment of sin. But, as for the Jewish refugee, freedom means not just escaping but finding somewhere to live. The Jewish refugee's ancestors escaped from Egypt, but the escape itself was not enough— as they frequently complained to Moses when they wandered in the desert. Freedom and safety from Egyptian oppression involved not only getting away from Egypt but also reaching the Promised Land; otherwise the escape was pointless—indeed worse than useless since slavery in Egypt was better than starving in the desert.

The person, then, who comes to a realization of his enslavement to sin and a belief that in Jesus Christ lies the possibility of liberation, cannot just stop there. To escape from his situation of alienation, such a person certainly takes the first step out of slavery by believing that Jesus is the Savior who has died to pay the necessary ransom for the human race. To reach freedom requires more than that. It is not enough to seize the chance of escaping. The escape to be successful demands somewhere safe to go. This place, this Promised Land, is the Church. The liberation Christ offers the human race consists not merely of recognizing that He is the Moses who can lead us out of the oppression to which our sinfulness has reduced us; it also includes following Him into the place in which He has prepared for us to live freely and safely.

It is this Catholic (and Orthodox) conviction, about the absolute importance of the Church in Christianity, which accounts for so many of the disputes and misunderstandings which bedevil relations with Protestants. So often the points of dispute are obscured by this basic divide which is not properly recognized as the real area of difference. The fact that the Church is not and cannot be claimed to be a utopia, but only the Promised Land of Christ, adds a further source of incomprehension. A Church which asserts her unfailing holiness but which, in fact, on this earth is made up of more or less sinful people, is going to be a Church which will be a sign of contradiction for many. And even without the blemishes which Catholics paradoxically claim cannot deprive the Church of her holiness, the Church still remains a complicated amalgam of both human and divine elements. Not surprisingly, Catholicism presents a very enigmatic face to many people, often simultaneously attractive and repellent.

Chapter 11

The Bogey of Infallibility

If you say that somebody thinks he is "infallible," the implication is that that person imagines he has all the answers on any subject on which he cares to pontificate. Of course, one can always modify such a criticism, as often occurs, by saying, for example, "When it comes to religion, he thinks he is infallible."

Well, there is someone about whom that comment could be made: the pope. And, as we turn now to a subject which has generated a great deal of confusion, we need to be clear what is *not* meant by the Catholic concept of infallibility. It emphatically does not mean that the pope is omniscient or that the Church is some sort of oracle of all truth, with ready answers to every question that can be asked. The popular usage of the word is really very unfortunate because it so easily does give the wrong impression: if it is impossible to err, to make a mistake, doesn't that imply one knows all the answers?

What the Catholic Church understands by infallibility—and it is a pity we cannot find another word—is something essentially negative rather than positive. In the first place, it means protection from error, not the capacity always to be right about everything. Secondly, this protection from error is absolutely limited to one area and one area alone: the transmission and interpretation of what has been revealed in and by Christ. This presupposes that this revelation was made to the Church rather than committed to a book or books called the Bible. This point suggests another distinction that has to be made. Infallibility belongs to people, not to things like writings.

It is true that the Catholic Church believes in what is called the "inspiration" of Scripture—but inspiration is not the same as infallibility. The writers of the New Testament were in a unique position of putting down the truth about Jesus Christ under the special influence of the Holy Spirit. Later popes have never been in that situation, any more than bishops, who are understood by the Catholic Church to be the descendants of the apostles, have actually witnessed the Resurrection, or, for that matter, have actually met Jesus in His earthly life. Nor does inspiration strictly belong to the writings, but rather to the writers themselves. The actual texts were not literally dictated by God. They were written by human beings employing human resources that were available to them in their time and culture. They have to be understood and interpreted in light of their background. In that sense there is nothing divine or supernatural about the scriptural writings. What alone makes them different from other literary texts is that, while they consist of human words, these human words express the divine Word of God. They are human words, but also God's Word. Inspired by the Spirit, who is the Spirit of truth, the writers put down the essential truths of revelation, those things which people need to know as pertaining to their liberation by Christ. The Bible, then, can be called a sacred book, but it is not sacred in the sense that its words fell out of heaven or that the words are unearthly utterances which cannot be subjected to ordinary methods of interpretation.

Just as inspiration, then, pertains to the writers rather than the writings, so infallibility attaches to the teachers rather than the teachings. This distinction may seem a bit academic, but it is not without significance. The reason is that if you start speaking of infallible dogmatic propositions, you then can easily slip into thinking that these statements are supposed to fall, as it were, out of heaven, or that the pope has a sort of hotline to God. Or, to put it in a less simplistic way, you may be tempted to regard these doctrinal pronouncements as somehow different from other human assertions in the sense of being exempt from normal linguistic and cultural conditions. You may be led into thinking of them as unchangeable in their formulation, not subject to history and time. Certainly some of the critics of the Catholic idea of infallibility have been guilty of this misunderstanding.

So what exactly is the Catholic understanding of infallibility? If allegedly definitive doctrines are not infallible, what are they? Well, they are *true*. That is not the same as being infallible. Words can't be incapable of being in error, only persons can be. Words, though, can state something which is true. If I say, "I am sitting at my desk," that is a true statement, but it doesn't make any sense to say that it is an "infallible" statement. It would, however, *make sense* to say that I am speaking infallibly. However, although the claim is meaningful, it is not in fact true. I am certainly in a very good position indeed to state that I am sitting at my desk, but that is not because I am infallible. Obviously, one doesn't have to be infallible to say things that are true. I know that I am sitting at my desk at the moment because I know I am, not because I am incapable of making mistakes. Of course, the truth of what I say depends on my not being insane or a liar, but if those two conditions are met, then I am the person who ought to know that I am sitting at my desk and it is unreasonable to ask me to prove it by, for example, calling in a witness. So that's the first thing we need to be clear about: you don't have to be infallible to say things that are true, nor, if you say something that is true, does that mean that you are infallible.

Now we are entitled to be believed when we say things which we are in a position to know, not because we are infallible, in general or on any particular subject, but because we have the facts before us, because we are so situated as to know. If you say that I could be mistaken in saying that I am sitting at my desk, I would have to conclude either that you were being facetious or that you thought I might be drunk or having hallucinations. Otherwise there is absolutely no reason why you should doubt my word, and if I am telling you on the telephone then you should be able to tell from my voice that I am perfectly sober and sane. But when it comes to other areas, there is no reason at all why you should believe what I say.

Well, then, what about truth in the area of religion? One approach to that question is to take the line that religion isn't a matter of truth, like the fact that when I am sitting at my desk then I cannot be standing at my desk or that two plus two equals four. According to this view, which is by no means uncommon, when someone speaks of what he believes, he may fondly suppose that he is saying something that is true, but it is only true *for himself*, not necessarily true for anyone else. This totally relative view of religious statements has come about chiefly because of the huge advances in scientific knowledge since the nineteenth century. In this intellectual climate people consciously or unconsciously think that any proposition, which claims to be true, must, if it is not logically true, conform to scientific criteria. In fact, as we have already seen, if one does take this highly circumscribed view of what can be called true, then the same objection that applies to the "truth" of religious belief also applies to a huge number of other things that we unhesitatingly state as though they were true—even though we couldn't begin to prove them in any kind of conventional scientific way. Indeed, as I have already pointed out, if this skeptical approach to religion is correct, then all the beliefs and convictions that are most personally important and dear to us are also just as uncertain as the religious ones. Thus if a man says, "I know my wife loves me," he expects others to see that statement as objectively true, even though he can't provide a scientific proof.

If this bogus concept, which identifies truth as relative, is accepted, then there is no point at all in such a doctrine as infallibility, since there is no longer any acceptance of objective truth, unless it is logically true or scientifically verifiable. But if we take the view that religious convictions are no different in their "truth-status" from a host of other convictions we confidently hold, then infallibility does make a lot of sense.

If we are asked to believe that something is true, which we can't verify for ourselves because we are not in a position to know, we need some kind of a reason to accept what we are told. In the case of somebody who tells us that, in spite of whatever rumors we may have heard, it is not true that her husband doesn't love her, we will accept this denial if, for example, we have a sufficient knowledge of the characters of the people involved. If we have good reason to know that the people spreading the rumors are malicious gossips, for instance, we will have an initial reluctance to believe their story against the husband. Or if we know the couple involved intimately and have seen their love for each other, then we will have a very good reason for treating the rumors, however well-attested, with considerable suspicion. So, when it comes to religious beliefs, beliefs about things which we have never witnessed for ourselves, how are we to be sure that what we are asked to believe is true?

Without going into nuances, we can say that there are three answers which those who call themselves Christians can make to this question. First, sadly, there are those in the churches that date from the Reformation who have been so deeply influenced by the relativist approach to non-logical, non-scientific statements which I have been describing that they are uncertain, to put it most mildly, that one can really talk about anything being absolutely and objectively true in Christianity. For the Bible and traditional Christian teachings offer a guide, but human knowledge grows and cultures change so that at the end of the day Christians can only use their own reason to determine what is true, or rather what makes sense for them in the particular age in which they live. Obviously, for this type of liberal Protestant, the whole notion of infallibility makes no sense at all. But let us be clear about this. It is not infallibility which is really the issue but the concept of objective truth in religion.

Then, there are those Protestants who assert that the Bible contains all the truths that Christians have to believe, that Scripture, which is inspired by God, is the sole authority which we must follow. Although this kind of Christian would be most unlikely to use the word "infallible"—and rightly so because, as we have seen, a book or writing cannot itself be infallible—nevertheless there is here a clear acceptance not only of objective truth but also of the idea of an unerring authority. The problems with this approach have already been mentioned. First, the New Testament itself witnesses to a Church which proclaims the Gospel through the apostles not through a book which was only in the process of being written. That is to say, it is the Church, the community "inspired" by the Holy Spirit, which teaches the Christian faith, not a collection of texts. Further, the writings of the New Testament, like those of the Old Testament, presuppose a people or community to interpret them, since no book can speak for itself, any more than it can open itself, or read itself.

Third, there is the Catholic (and Orthodox) view that Scripture is certainly of unique importance, but so also is Tradition. Tradition is witnessed to by the New Testament itself, where it is clearly understood, explicitly as well as implicitly, that it does not contain everything that is known and believed by the Church. The gospel writers, as well as Saint Paul, make no secret of the fact that they are not attempting to put down everything on paper. How could they? The Gospels do not pretend to be full biographies or historical accounts of the life of Jesus. They are much better described—as indeed they are by one of the second-century Fathers who has left us an unforgettable description of a celebration of the Eucharist in the early Church—as memoirs, that is to say, partial and selective memories. And as for Saint Paul, he is after all only writing letters, which, like all letters, relate to specific issues concerning the particular people to whom he is writing. He is certainly not attempting to write a detailed handbook or manual containing everything Christians have to believe. Surely the poor man would be horrified to think that his surviving letters would be treated in any such way. In which case, like the gospel writers, he could have been expected to do a rather better job. Indeed, instead of spending so much time traveling around and frequently talking about it, he should have shut himself up in his study and spent all his time getting down on paper everything that he had heard and knew. A moment's reflection shows that, if we exaggerate the role of Scripture, we are faced with the embarrassing fact that the apostles made what can only be called an absolute hash of things. Why on earth, in particular, did they not sit down with Saint Paul and try to compose a compendium of Christianity? In other words, those first Christians were receiving the Gospel of Christ *orally*, and what they heard is more than what we have written down for us. Tradition means both the act of handing down or transmitting and that which is handed down or transmitted. Clearly what the apostles passed on was not only what they said but also what they did. The faith, life, and worship of the first generation of Christians, who did not have the New Testament in front of them, were handed on to the next generation who in turn transmitted it to the next. This is what is meant by Tradition, which is closely connected with the New Testament writings which ultimately come from the same Source.

The Catholic understanding is that neither Scripture nor Tradition can be separated from the Church, to which both belong. For it is the Church which has been entrusted by Christ with the job of interpreting and teaching the faith, the revelation contained in

Scripture and Tradition. Now, if this is the case, then the members of the Church need to have some sort of guarantee that what they are told is indeed authentic, true to what the apostles originally passed on. And this is what is referred to by this rather unfortunate word "infallible." For what was revealed to the apostles by Jesus and the Holy Spirit was strictly limited. They were not given some kind of divine insight into the secrets of the universe. What they knew was strictly limited, limited to Jesus Christ as they had experienced Him in His earthly and risen life, and as the Spirit had also enlightened them. Jesus had told them the Spirit would lead them into the whole truth, but by that He didn't mean all human knowledge. The knowledge they possessed was strictly restricted to knowledge of Jesus Christ, the Word of God.

Now the Church from the earliest times, as we discussed earlier, showed an extraordinary confidence in making certain crucial decisions, like electing somebody to replace the traitor Judas Iscariot. According to the record, there was no hesitation at all as to whether they should replace him or how they should do it. Again, the decision that non-Jewish converts should not be expected to become Jews as part and parcel of being Christians was apparently taken quite decisively. In other words, the apostles had no doubt that they had both the authority to make such decisions and that there was no danger in their making a mistake. The written records reveal no hesitation either before or after the decisions were taken. Considering all the doubts and hesitations that persisted up to the Ascension, as we have seen, it is quite remarkable how after Pentecost, not only is the apostles' faith in Jesus Christ absolute and impregnable, but also their confidence in the authority and power they had been given strikes the reader of the New Testament as remarkably serene.

Jesus' promise to the apostles that the Spirit would lead them into all truth implies that He certainly had a concept of objective truth. In view of His mandate to them to go out and teach the world this truth, He must have intended that this truth would endure beyond their deaths, in just the same way as His solemn injunction to the apostles to do what He had done at the Last Supper in memory of Him, or His commission to Peter, would have been pretty pointless if these instructions were only intended to last during their lifetimes. This, at any rate, was how the Church in succeeding generations understood

His words. So if the truth about Jesus Christ was meant to endure and to last, then presumably the Church must have some guarantee that it will not in fact lose or distort anything of what the apostles communicated. Such a guarantee, which seems essential if the mission of Jesus Christ is not to be aborted, is only possible if the Church has actually been endowed with some faculty or power to ensure that it would not lapse into confusion and error over its teaching.

As with other Christian doctrines, as we have seen, if the infallibility of the Church was not part of its inheritance we should really have to invent it. It is not that the Church has to be all-knowing, omniscient. It is not part of the Church's function, for example, to be making scientific discoveries. But it is the responsibility of the Church, presumably, to keep careful hold over what has been passed on to her if it is to have any credibility. This is where infallibility has to come in. The Church must enjoy a certain freedom from the possibility of making a mistake in any essential matter. Otherwise there is no reason why anybody should listen to her.

As ages and cultures succeed each other, the Church has to go on communicating its message, but inevitably this message has to undergo some change, but without losing its meaning. After all, the Church on earth is not isolated or preserved from contact with historical changes. The Church herself consists of living human beings, albeit drawing spiritual life from the Spirit. She is not cocooned, sheltered from the changes in the culture and society in which her members live. Words, for instance, alter their sense. New problems, new questions arise. The very first Christians were not immediately faced by difficulties that later generations found in conceiving how Jesus could be both human and divine. Inevitably, some people came to stress one side or the other: if Jesus were *really* God, then how could He be a man as well? Or if He *were* a man, then how could He also be God?

Fallen human beings have fallen human minds. They are likely to be impatient with the supernatural truths that their limited finite minds cannot readily grasp. Human beings are prone to the fault of exaggerating. They see one aspect of the truth, which they want to highlight regardless of other aspects which they may not have appreciated. As a result, it is very easy for caricatures rather than the full picture of the truth to be drawn. These caricatures are what are called heresies, a word which comes from a Greek word meaning choosing or selecting. In other words, a certain element or elements are picked out in such a way as to obscure others just as a cartoonist caricatures a well-known figure by emphasizing certain prominent features at the expense of other less noticeable features. In the resulting cartoon we recognize the person caricatured but we know it is not a true resemblance. It is these caricatures of doctrine which heretics, often well-meaning people, produce through the ages. Thus, in the sixteenth century, the fact that Jesus used bread and wine at the Last Supper, which He instructed His apostles to eat and drink, was taken to mean that the bread and wine of the Eucharist must really just be symbolic, anything else being mere superstition. In response, the Catholic Church had to say that while it was certainly true that the bread and wine remained bread and wine in the Eucharist so far as sight and taste were concerned, nevertheless fidelity to the words of Jesus demanded that this bread and wine became His Body and Blood in a very real, not merely symbolic, sense.

We all know that life demands that we are continually changing in all sorts of ways. It is true that we can resist change, but paradoxically if we do dig our heels in and refuse to adapt to new factors and changing circumstances we end up strangely enough not retaining whatever it is we didn't want to be changed. If, for example, we refuse ever to buy a new car, then as the years go by we will find that we no longer have the same smart up-to-date car which we originally bought. We will have, rather, an antique or vintage car, which may indeed have its attractions, but they are not the same features which originally appealed to us when we bought it. Or again, fashions in clothes change, and if we persist in never changing our wardrobe, those clothes that once looked perfectly normal come to look old-fashioned and give us an eccentric appearance. Perhaps the clothes haven't changed much physically, but the signal they give is now a completely different one. If someone suffers from a Peter Pan syndrome and refuses to grow up, sadly his childhood does not last, but he becomes a childish adult, very different from the real child he once was. To absolutely refuse to change means fossilization, as there is no way things can remain absolutely the same—or rather they can in one sense remain the same but not without losing their original character or identity. It is true of individuals; it is true of communities and peoples and institutions. And it is, therefore, not surprising that it is also true of the Church.

Not only, as it has famously been remarked, is it true that to live is to change, but also it is necessary to change in order to remain the same. But if a living, as opposed to a fossilized, Church has, then, inevitably to undergo change as circumstances and situations alter in the course of history, a problem arises. Take, for instance, a country like the United States where there is a written constitution, which no more speaks for itself than the Bible can. Consequently, there is a Supreme Court which ultimately decides whether something is unconstitutional or not. When this highest authority makes a ruling on a constitutional matter, this judgment then becomes part of a whole body of interpretation and understanding of what the Constitution means. A development has taken place in American constitutional history. The Supreme Court does not, naturally, claim to be infallible but it does have the last word against which there is no appeal. Otherwise, if there was no recognized arbiter, there then would be nothing to stop the American legislative and executive branches, as well as the various judiciaries, from acting in whatever unconstitutional ways they chose. In other words, somebody has to decide what the Constitution means as new issues and questions arise.

In the case of the Church where God's self-revelation is concerned, there must be some authority capable of deciding whether particular changes in doctrine are authentic developments, which are not only true to the original revelation but actually supportive of and vital for the safe preservation of the revelation. If this is so, then Jesus' promise to the disciples that the Spirit would lead them into all truth takes on added significance. For His promise is made not only to the original Apostles but to their intended successors. If, as common sense suggests, Jesus' instructions were not intended to die with the death of the apostles, then His promise clearly applies to the Church and its leaders in subsequent ages. And this is all that the infallibility of the Church means.

So how does the controversial issue of papal infallibility fit into this? Well, it means that the pope is infallible in exactly the same way that the Church is. He is certainly not omniscient, nor is he inspired like the writers of Scripture. It is simply that on very specific occasions he has the authority to define a particular doctrine not because he believes it but because the Church believes it: that is, he declares what the faith of the Church is. But what if it isn't the faith of the Church? There can only be two answers to that question. In the unlikely event of the pope going insane, then obviously he would be removed from office as mentally unfit. But otherwise, one can only say what one can only say about any other Christian doctrine: namely, that one believes it because the Church says so. And here the Catholic is really in no different situation from any Christian who thinks that one discovers what Christianity is from reading the Bible. For after all, why should one believe what the Bible says, or appears to say? Again, there can only be one answer to that: because one believes that the Bible tells the truth. In other words, one trusts the authority of the Bible. If somebody refuses to believe in the authority and truth of the Bible, then the Bible Christian has no option except to appeal to faith or to try and argue for the truth of the Bible on the basis of reason. And this is also all that the Catholic can do. In short, there is no reason why one should believe in the Trinity because one believes the doctrine to be in the Bible or because, as I have suggested, it makes sense of the idea of a loving personal God—but then refuse to believe in infallibility which one can also argue for from Scripture and the nature of a revelation which claims to be objectively true.

Before ending this chapter I must add three points. First, as I have said, the infallibility of the pope is not personal in the sense of being exclusive to him: it is simply the infallibility of the Church. The whole Church, led by the Spirit, possesses this inability to make any serious mistakes concerning Jesus Christ, so far as He has been revealed to the Church. But only one part of the Church has the competence to speak authoritatively, and that is the hierarchy of pope and bishops who are the successors to the apostles. It is, of course, not only the pope who can infallibly define a point of faith. In the vast majority of cases this has been done by Councils involving not just a group of local bishops but the whole body of bishops, including always the senior bishop, the pope, who has to authenticate and endorse whatever decisions are made by the particular Council.

CHAPTER 12

HOW THE CHURCH
GROWS WITH DEATH

G. K. Chesterton once remarked that the Church is the only human community which actually grows rather than diminishes as its members die, because not only do new members join but the dead do not cease to be members of the Church. The Catholic view is that death is not the end of a human life but, rather, the end of earthly life and the beginning of a new life. In this new life the person still belongs to the Church which is the People of God and the Body of Christ. What changes is his condition or situation as he is now in a different part of the Church. But he is not separated from those on earth in the sense of being cut off from any mutual communication. What does this mean?

At the Reformation Protestantism lost the links between the dead and the living by rejecting both purgatory and "praying to the saints." The Reformers regarded both as encouraging superstition and undermining the key doctrine that Christians are "justified" or saved by their faith. If somebody believes in Christ then that person is saved and must go straight to heaven when he dies. To suggest otherwise would be to cast doubt on the victory Christ has won over death and sin by dying on the Cross for us: all that human beings are now required to do is to put their faith in this all-powerful atonement which can then be applied to, or take effect personally for, the individual believer. There are, therefore, only two destinations open to the dead person—heaven if he believes that Christ is his savior and hell if he rejects Christ. If this is the case, then there are no dead people for whom to pray for in purgatory (since it doesn't exist) and no point (to put it mildly) in asking those in heaven to pray for us, as if they can do something for us which our own faith cannot do.

Now, regardless of whether or not Protestantism is right, the fact is that the rejection of these two Catholic and, of course, Orthodox beliefs meant the end of any real link between the dead and the living. Those in heaven can't—and shouldn't—do anything for us which we can't do for ourselves, so it is useless and wrong to ask for their prayers as though God will listen to them rather than to us, when it is our faith alone which can save us (we can't shift the responsibility on to anyone else). And equally, since there is no such place or condition as purgatory where people are purified of their imperfections, there is no earthly point in us praying for nonexistent people in a nonexistent place or condition. As one historian of the Reformation has remarked, the lines of community were redrawn in the sixteenth century, in the sense of being hugely narrowed. The dead were now beyond the reach of human contact and communication. They could no longer affect those still on earth, so there was absolutely no use in praying to them in the sense of asking for their prayers. There was, likewise, no purpose in praying for them as though we, as opposed to Christ, could do anything to help them. It would be vain and blasphemous for us to think that we could in any way affect their welfare. The boundaries of community had indeed drastically shrunk. So far as Christians on earth were concerned, the dead were literally the departed. They were no longer there to help or to be helped. They were simply dead and gone and that was that. One could only hope they had gone to the right place.

Now, if we leave aside for the moment the question of purgatory and the point of asking those in heaven to pray for us, we surely need to be clear as to what kind of a place or condition heaven is—or, to put it differently, what it means to be saved. As we have already seen, Catholic Christianity is consistent with the nature of human existence in stressing both the absolute value of the individual, who cannot be reduced to a unit in a mass, and also the undeniably social character of life in which no person can exist as an isolated individual. In the Church, the individual member personally is empowered with the Holy Spirit, but this only happens through the agency of the Church of which that person becomes a member precisely by being endowed with the Spirit. As in life, so in the Church, the individual has to be a member of the community, but equally the community is made up of individuals. When, then, we think about being saved and getting to heaven, we would expect the same situation to prevail. After all, would we want to be saved all by ourselves? Would we want to inhabit happily ever after our own little corner of heaven away from everybody else? What sort of a heaven would that be? It would surely be a pretty good way of imagining hell, cut off from the love of our fellow human beings.

No, heaven, if it means anything, must mean happiness, and happiness for human beings is loving and being loved. If there is also a personal God who loves us, then heaven must also mean possessing His love in all its fullness and returning it. Any kind of individualistic salvation just doesn't make sense if one is a human being, let alone a Christian. Heaven must mean both being fully oneself *and* being fully in harmony with others, as well as with God. God creates us as unique individuals, but when we are created we become members of the human race. This situation is exactly reflected when somebody becomes a member of the Church. It must also be true of heaven.

There is a famous, or notorious, Catholic doctrine, which is often a source of embarrassment to Catholics, to the effect that there is no salvation outside the Church. Now it is perfectly true that this doctrine was often in the past understood in a very exclusivist sense. But, as always, we need to remember that this, like any other doctrine, has to be interpreted. It is one thing to say that only Catholics can be saved, and quite another to say that no one can be saved apart from the Church. If, for instance, I am drowning and am pulled out of the water unconscious, I am not in a position to know who my rescuer is. Similarly, one can be saved by Christ without knowing it. Since being saved by Christ involves being a member of His Church, everyone who is saved must somehow belong to the Church, albeit at times unknowingly. Certainly, all those in heaven must be part of the People of God, which is the Church. There is really no alternative to the doctrine of no salvation outside the Church if one believes that Jesus Christ is the Savior of the world and if one also understands that that salvation comes to the individual personally, not collectively. However, at the same time, salvation comes not in an individualistic way but in and through the community, which Jesus has endowed with His Spirit. The fact that the doctrine may have been understood in a much more literal and narrower sense by Catholics in the past only goes to show, first, that doctrine is one thing, interpretation another, and, second, that the Church develops under the influence of the Spirit in its understanding of the truth entrusted to it.

So how can a person be saved through Christ's Church without knowing it? Well, just as a person can owe his life to someone whom he may never even see or know his name, so too a person's life can be saved by a number of people whom he may never know. If a group of people can save an individual, so too can a larger community by, for example, agreeing to grant asylum to a refugee in danger of death. Someone may desperately need a transit visa through one country to reach safety in another, but the fact that that person may never leave the aircraft or airport and never see or know anything of that country which has granted him the visa on which his life depends, doesn't affect the reality that it is this country, which has given him a means of escape. To put it in a different way, someone can live in a country and never actually become a citizen, although in spirit he is really a citizen of that country and not the country whose passport he carries. Jesus Himself pointed out that those who were not against Him were for Him. The "good thief" executed beside Him is promised entry into heaven, although his knowledge of and faith in Jesus was somewhat limited, to say the least.

We must now return to the question of the legitimacy of praying to the saints. And we need to be clear from the start who the saints are. There are certain men and women who have been formally declared by the Church to be saints, whose prayers Catholics are recommended to request. These saints, whose statues may be put up in churches, are only, as it were, the tip of the iceberg. For the saints are all those who are in heaven, and Catholics may ask anyone they believe to be in heaven to pray for them. The only difference with the canonized saints is that the Church guarantees that they are in heaven and highlights their lives as eminently worthy of imitation.

But if the saints are not prayed to as God is, as the Father and the Son and the Holy Spirit are, what is the point of asking for *their* prayers rather than making one's request known directly to God? Is it not rather an unnecessary and roundabout way of doing things? Much worse, doesn't it give the impression that God is not all-powerful and doesn't it appear to sideline Jesus who is the sole Savior? Is it not distracting, not to say blasphemous, to be using third parties, so to speak, when Jesus Himself told us to address God as our Father?

These objections may seem rather plausible until we reflect that this would go against our ever asking anyone for their prayers. Why should a sick Christian request or accept prayers on his behalf, when he can go straight to God, directly through Jesus? What is the point, let alone the justification, of such a proceeding? And yet I have never heard of anyone taking that attitude, however anti-Catholic he may be. It is such a natural, normal thing to do. To object to someone praying for one is surely extraordinary, indeed inhuman. To say that to accept or ask for prayers from other people is superstitious or lacking in faith is bizarre. After all, the one prayer that Jesus taught His disciples involves praying for others: He didn't say that I should pray to my Father for my daily bread, for His forgiveness of *my* sins as I forgive those who sin against me, and so on. No, the prayer He instituted is strictly communal—I have to pray not only for my bread but for the bread of others ("give us *our* daily bread") and so on. Praying for others, or intercessory prayer, is common to both the Old and New Testaments. Anyone with the slightest religious feelings or instincts understands it perfectly well. So if praying for others is such a natural thing to do, quite apart from any belief in Christianity, why should not those in heaven pray for those on earth? Jesus Himself prayed for His disciples. Are we to suppose that those who now enjoy full loving communion with God and their fellow human beings have no interest in those on earth? To object that the saints, that is, those in heaven are perfectly happy to leave God to look after those on earth flies in the face of all that we have said about why Christ established a new People of God, a new "assembly," His Church: He wanted human cooperation in the same way that God intended when He made man in His image. From the original People of God He chose particular individuals to further His design, just as He used the chosen people itself. Employing human instruments is integral to God's dealings with the human race according to the Bible. Therefore, in heaven it is hardly likely that God would not want the saints to cooperate through their prayers.

As well as abolishing the allegedly corrupt and superstitious practice of "praying to the saints," the Reformation also dismissed the idea of purgatory as incompatible with being saved by faith in Christ. If the Bible taught that Jesus had saved sinners by atoning on the Cross and if all that sinners need—and could—do was to accept in faith the salvation offered gratuitously to them, then what else could be needed to gain entry into heaven? What could be more repugnant to the conviction that helpless sinners could do nothing of any merit on their own, and that all that counted was Christ's atonement than the idea that the prayers of these very sinners could help the dead who were in purgatory? The whole doctrine smacked of human pride and faithlessness.

In response, let us consider for a moment what we mean by being saved. Suppose, to take my earlier example, I am saved from drowning and dragged out of the water onto dry land. If I really were going to die, then I would be in pretty bad shape after being taken from the water. If I had been in my clothes, then these would be in very sad state, while physically I would be very much the worse for wear, to say the least. It would take me some time to recover. I might even have to go to the hospital for treatment; there might be a long period of convalescence. But I think I should be very surprised if somebody came to visit me in hospital and, on seeing my weak condition, remarked with disappointment, "Oh, I was under the impression that you had been saved from drowning." I would indeed have been saved, but that is quite a different thing from being in good shape. If I were fighting in a battle and was wounded, I might be carried to safety, but that would not change the fact that I was still wounded.

Being saved by Christ, therefore, does not necessarily mean that one is ready to enter heaven. To change the analogy, I may get an invitation to meet a very important and famous person, but that doesn't mean that I don't first have to make some preparations for the encounter, such as, for example, reading the celebrity's books if he is a well-known author. However, the fact that I may need time to make myself ready for the meeting doesn't in any way imply that I have not been invited or that the invitation has been withdrawn. Similarly, to be invited into heaven doesn't exclude the possibility that first I need to be in a fit state.

To be forgiven my sins by Christ doesn't remove the scars and stains left by my sins nor the continuing existence of bad inclinations which sinful habits create in me. The sediment of sin, one might say, doesn't disappear, any more than my forgiving somebody a wrong they have committed against me means that somehow the wrong just ceases to exist. For if I simply forget the offense, then I can hardly be said to forgive, since there is nothing to forgive in that case. Nor does forgiving, as people sometimes seem to imagine, mean that I decide that the other person really didn't do what I know they did do. In that case again, there would then be no forgiving to do as there would be no real wrong any longer to forgive. No, the reason why forgiving is so difficult is precisely because one doesn't forget, because a real offense has been committed. The same is true of our sins. God can't just forget them or brush them aside or pretend they don't exist.

Anyway, if He did do that, as I remarked earlier, He would not be taking us seriously as responsible human beings. What God can do is to forgive us. That is to say, He doesn't forget or ignore our sins, but He does not hold them against us in the sense of wishing to do us harm. He does not refuse to acknowledge us any more. He is ready to resume the relationship which he has always wanted to have with us ever since creating us. That is what forgiveness is all about.

And so, yes, God forgives us, but we still have to make amends. This is also true of human life.

A husband who has been unfaithful to his wife may ask and receive her forgiveness, but it would be a very poor kind of repentance if that husband just breathed a sigh of relief and said, "Oh, good; I knew you wouldn't really mind, so we can just carry on where we left off." For surely a husband in that situation, who was genuinely sorry, would not at all be content to be left off the hook in that easy way. Far from expecting his wife to carry on as if nothing amiss had ever happened, he would be the first to want to make amends, to try and do something that would make up for his infidelity—not because he thought it would simply remove the hurt done to his wife, which he can never do, but because he would want to show her both how truly sorry he was, and also how anxious he was to put himself out by way of penance. Of course, it may well be that really sincere sorrow on the part of the husband may lead to their love for each other actually increasing. They both may want in the aftermath to say that the breach he has caused has, in fact, led to good. Well, we have already seen how that is true in the case of the "happy fault" of Adam and Eve. But it would still be very odd indeed, to say the least, if that unfaithful husband were to exclaim to his forgiving wife, "I'm so glad now that I committed adultery!—Aren't you?"

God, then, does take sin very seriously indeed, just as He takes us very seriously, modeled in our nature as we are on Him. That is why He cannot just pat us on the head and casually say, "Oh, don't worry, I quite understand." God does, of course, understand perfectly well why we sin, but He also deplores it deeply, not only because all sin is a slap in His face, but because He knows, even better than we know, how fatally sin destroys our happiness and well-being. Moreover, although indeed our sins can be forgiven by God, there are, unfortunately, consequences to our sinning which He cannot ignore.

To return to our example, the unfaithful husband has seriously damaged a relationship, so that his wife's trust in him has been undermined. He needs to try to restore this trust which is essential for both his and her peace of mind. In other words, the husband has not merely done something of which he is now ashamed but which can somehow be set to one side as having no connection with anything else. Even though he may never have done anything like that before, it is still not an isolated act. But just as, in the famous saying, no man is an island, we are all interconnected members of the human race, so too our actions are never without consequences and effects. In the case of adultery between married people *at least* four people are involved. Moreover, the unfaithful husband has not merely damaged others, he has also damaged himself and not only in his relationship with them. By a single sexual transgression, he may very well, for example, have made it easier for him to do it again. Habits are not born out of nothing, they are created by single acts, if we trace them back. Again, the husband may by this one affair have destroyed his confidence in his own self-control, or in his sense of his own commitment and loyalty, or in his certainty that he does really love his wife.

When the unfaithful husband confesses to his wife and asks her forgiveness, the fact of being forgiven is not the end of the matter if the husband's contrition is serious and sincere. It is still very much the beginning of the healing or purification process. If one genuinely regrets something one has done, one has a natural desire to be punished. Well, the husband's punishment begins with his distress at what he has done, continues with his humiliation in having to confess and, then, with his pain in seeing how much he has hurt his wife. To show how sorry he is, he will put himself out in a special way to try and make amends. But, thereafter, there will always be this shadow of the past, even if never alluded to, over their life together, even if there are also positive effects as well. As I have said, there are the consequences and implications of the adultery to add to the husband's punishment.

Now the reason I have been rather laboring all this is to explain what the Catholic belief about purgatory actually is. There are many, including no doubt Catholics with a poor understanding of their faith, who imagine that it is a place where God punishes sinners in the sort of way that society punishes criminals by sending them to prison. Using this analogy, one's "time" in purgatory will depend on how bad one's sins were on earth. There are two reasons why this analogy conveys a completely false idea of purgatory.

First of all, to imagine purgatory as a sort of prison is like imagining heaven to be a place where one will be able to enjoy all the things one most enjoyed in life but to eternal and total satisfaction. If, for example, one's idea of "heaven"—the very word people use— is, say, basking on a beach in the Bahamas, then that is what God will provide in heaven. Since different people enjoy different things, presumably there will also be in heaven wonderful mountains and snow for those who prefer skiing to sunbathing—and so on. Well, that, of course, is an absurd and puerile misrepresentation of what is meant by heaven, where happiness is defined in terms of love not material pleasure. But, strange to say, there are many people who do materialize spiritual realities in this bizarre way. So, for them, purgatory is some sort of a penitentiary or prison, where the inmates are deprived of most of the pleasures of life. Hell, on the other hand, is presumably assumed to be a sort of vast concentration camp, with the disadvantage that one never is actually sent to the gas chamber, which would at least terminate the suffering and torture. It is not surprising that so many people in a modern secular society, who pride themselves on being educated, dismiss Christianity, and particularly Catholicism, as utterly unbelievable, when they display such childish ideas about its doctrines.

The second way in which the idea of some sort of prison trivializes the Catholic concept of purgatory is that it suggests that God "sends" us to purgatory against our will, since if there is anyone in prison who has actually asked to go there, then that person must be very much the exception to the general rule. Purgatory, however, which means purification certainly involves punishment, but the punishment is not externally imposed on the unwilling soul. One "goes" to purgatory because one wants to—just as somebody with cancer wants the painful treatment which is the only hope he has of surviving. I don't know of anyone who enjoys going to the dentist, but I also don't know of anyone who wouldn't want to go if he had a raging toothache. In both these examples the proffered treatment involves pain, but obviously only a masochist goes for the pain. Nor, on the other hand, is the doctor or dentist guilty of sadism in inflicting the pain. It is not as though the patient is told, "If you want to be cured or healed, you must endure my sadistic pleasure." The only external pain which either the doctor or the dentist will impose is the cost of the treatment, if one has to pay privately for it oneself. So to imagine that God imposes purgatory on us as the price which He demands for entry into heaven, as though He insists on our being punished for the sins we have committed, is wholly to misunderstand the nature of purgatory. It is true that the Catholic Church recognizes a "penal" aspect to purgatory, but this should never be separated from the purification which is purgatory. Certainly, God is a God of justice, and certainly, as we have seen, Christ's atonement on the Cross paid the price or the ransom incurred by human sin which only He could pay. But Christ's death cancelled the debt; purgatory is not an additional punishment to propitiate the God of justice. The human race has been redeemed by Christ, and any suggestion that purgatory is a sort of extra to the price Christ paid on the Cross is not only a misrepresentation of what is meant by purgatory, but it is also not Christian.

So we need to be quite clear about this: insofar as there is a penal aspect to purgatory it is not in addition to the purification. No, purification is painful and therein lies the punishment. It hurts when one has to go to the doctor or to the hospital to have something infectious or malignant removed from one's body; one may indeed shrink from having it done, but one knows that the pain will be worth it. So what sort of painful purification can purgatory consist of? Well, the adulterous husband shrinks from the misery of having to confess to what he has done and dreads his wife's tears; her reproaches are bad enough, but even worse is the sight of her unhappiness. This is the worst punishment of all for the loving but unfaithful husband. He would much prefer it if she just got angry with him, as her anger is less terrible to him than her misery. He has to confess to her if he is to have a clear conscience and to receive her forgiveness. His confession is part of his purification, as are his humiliation and his constant sense of the pain he has caused his wife. It would be a huge relief to him if his wife would just punish him by imposing some punishment. That would be far more bearable than the mental agony. So one could well say that a trivialized idea of purgatory as a place of physical torture might actually be less truly painful than the spiritual purification which is the real purgatory.

There are stories of people who have been given up for dead but who don't, in fact, die. It is interesting that in some of the accounts of what they experienced there is memory of a very bright light. Traditionally, the Church has used the image of fire in connection with both hell and purgatory. By burning, fire lights and warms as well as burns. The sun can cause death, but it is also the source of life. A loving but unfaithful husband will find his cheeks burning with shame when he confesses to his wife. Love makes us glow with happiness, but it also burns when it is betrayed.

When we die we shall encounter the God who is Love directly, face-to-face, as it were. The light or the fire of His love which burns for us will have two painful effects for those who are in need of purification. It will light up our egotistical selfish lives as they have never been revealed before to us. What we glimpsed only partially, perhaps because we didn't want to see before, will now be illuminated by the all-powerful rays of God's love. That will be a painful experience—to see fully for the first time exactly what kind of people we were.

There will also be another dimension to the pain of seeing the light of God's love. Because we have become so used to preferring spiritual darkness to light we shall, most of us, find that light extremely painful to look at. We have all had the experience of sitting in a room on a summer's evening as the twilight gradually turns into night, and somebody switches on the light suddenly. Our eyes have adjusted to the darkness, and the unexpected electric light hurts them. But we know the light has to be put on, if, for instance, we are to enjoy a meal together. Well, in a similar sort of way when we die most of us will find the sun of God's love more or less hard to contemplate. We will need time to become accustomed to it, as well as time to face up without evasion to the real nature of our lives. This will be a more or less painful experience as we gradually open our eyes to the more or less (depending on how used to darkness we are) blinding light of God's love.

That is what purgatory is all about. Heaven will be when we can fully and longingly gaze at that light. As for hell, there must always be the possibility of somebody refusing to open his eyes and preferring the darkness of the ego.

CHAPTER 13

THE MOST IMPORTANT
MEMBER OF THE CHURCH

Needless to say, I am not referring to Jesus Christ in the title of this chapter. Christ is indeed the head of the Church, but He is not a member of it like I am. No, the person I am referring to is a member of the Church who is now in heaven, the woman who was His earthly mother when He was born into this world.

Now, as we know, even better than our ancestors, through our increased medical knowledge, the woman who conceives and gives birth to us is an immensely important figure in our lives. We begin our existence in and through her; our life starts inside her, and therefore we cannot help being affected for better or worse by her when we are in her womb. As I have often remarked in the course of this book, we are certainly unique individuals but we are also interconnected and interdependent as members of the human race. This is true from the beginning of our human life. We don't just arrive in this world, directly created by God. Our life depends on the sexual interaction of a male and a female.

When God joined the human race, He too came into this world as a result of female fertility. Being fully human, He, like the rest of us, was conceived in and born from a woman's womb. But, of course, if He was also fully God, we would surely expect Him not to come into this world exactly like us. There would presumably be a divine element also in His birth. This is what the New Testament says and what Catholic Christianity has always asserted. As one of the gospel writers puts it, He was not born as a result of the "urge of the flesh or will of man." In other words, the Incarnation did not depend on human initiative but on divine initiative. Although a woman was involved, a man was not. It was God's idea, God's plan, and therefore God had to make the crucial move. To this extent, Jesus' birth could not be a normal human birth. Certainly, it had to include the human factor if He was to be fully and really human. But it also had to include the divine factor if He was still to be fully and really God.

According to the two gospel writers (Luke 1:35-37, Matthew 1:18) who are most explicit and specific about the manner of His birth, Jesus was conceived in Mary's womb not as a result of sexual intercourse with her fiancé, Joseph, but as a result of her spiritual intercourse with the Holy Spirit. Since the Holy Spirit is above all the Love that is God, we could say that Mary was made pregnant by this divine Love. Indeed, one of the Gospels uses an image suggestive of sexual intercourse when it speaks of the Holy Spirit "coming upon" Mary.

When God created human beings in His image, He did not intend our sexuality to be something purely physical. We are certainly bodily beings who cannot escape from our bodies, and, therefore, we would expect reproduction to involve our physical bodies. We would also expect our minds or hearts to be involved, our emotions as well as our physical organs. Sexual intercourse between man and woman is necessarily physical, but intercourse as God intended it was to involve more than merely physical union. It was to be a union of hearts and minds as well as bodies. Human beings, if they were to be proper human beings, that is, true reflections of their Creator in whose image they were made, would by their very nature exercise their sexuality as an expression of love as well as physical instinct. The bodily desire to copulate was meant by God to go hand-in-hand with the mental and spiritual desire to achieve close loving union with another person.

When the Holy Spirit "came upon" Mary, God was not raping her spiritually, let alone physically as in pagan mythologies. This "intercourse" was free and loving; it required Mary's consent before it could happen. If Mary had said "no," then it would not have taken place. The fate of the human race depended on her "yes," just as it had once hung on whether the first woman, Eve, would say "yes" to God and "no" to the devil. In universal terms, Christianity puts woman, not man, as the key player on the two most momentous occasions in the history of the human race.

I said "Christianity," but I have to modify that because in the sixteenth century those Christians who "protested" against the Church included in their protest, as we have seen, what they regarded as the unscriptural cult of the saints. And, of course, far and away the most important of the saints is Mary. To ask Mary for her prayers, as though something was lacking in what her Son had accomplished, to approach Mary instead of going directly to Christ was regarded as against biblical Christianity. Anyway, apart from praying to Mary, to suggest in any way that she had played a crucial role in our liberation seemed to these protesters and their successors to imply that Christ Himself was not solely the cause of our salvation. As a result, Mary faded into the background. She became a historical figure—like all the dead, that is, the departed—although naturally she was still recognized as the Virgin Mary who had brought Jesus Christ into the world and who was naturally deserving of all admiration, honor, and respect. Although her memory still evoked more reverence than any other human being, she no longer entered into the faith of Protestants as the title she was given at one of the earliest Councils of the Church, the "Mother of God," implied.

Yes, certainly, she was the mother of Jesus and no doubt much less sinful than any other human being, but she came to be seen more as the biological channel—again, doubtless, the very best of channels that God could have chosen—but still a more or less passive (even though freely consenting) channel rather than an active agent. We now know from medical science that women don't, in fact, necessarily become pregnant if all the right biological conditions are present; everything may be in place, but if the woman is too stressed through her job, for example, then she may fail to get pregnant. The fact is that a woman is more active in conceiving or failing to conceive than used to be supposed.

Now, in the case of Mary, the Gospel account certainly doesn't say that God just asked her for the use of her body so that the Incarnation could be made possible, and that she, in any casual way, agreed. Her response to the news that she is to get pregnant through the Holy Spirit and that her child will be called the Son of God is couched in very solemn terms which make it clear that she agrees rather than submits. Her consent to what is to take place is based on her explicit readiness to do whatever God wants of her. If Mary had not concurred with God's will, then the Incarnation could not have taken place as it did. In other words, God, we can say without impugning His power, was dependent on a human being to carry out His plan. There is nothing strange about that. In creating human beings God wanted their cooperation in His design for them. When the human race refused to cooperate, God was frustrated, since, although all-powerful, even God can't have His cake and eat it. That is to say, He can't give us our freedom without letting us do what we want to do. After all, God can hardly talk nonsense or act in an utterly contradictory way.

As we have already seen, this desire on God's part for human cooperation explains why He gives such power to the new People of God, Christ's Church. He must have known the risk He ran. Well, we know He did because Jesus Himself experienced betrayal from one of His appointed apostles, and a little later was disowned by the man He had made the head apostle. Those people who are shocked by the corruptions—and there have been and are very real corruptions in the Catholic Church—obviously have not read the New Testament very carefully. It is ironic that the scandals which most shock people and are most commonly used as an excuse for not joining or staying in the Church relate to the papacy itself! Human beings can be very imperceptive and unimaginative. Here is the very first pope failing Jesus when the crisis came—and it did not come unexpectedly. Not only had Jesus warned His disciples very explicitly as to the fate He was to suffer, most specifically of all on the last night of His life on earth, but He'd actually predicted Peter's disloyalty, much to the indignation of Peter. Is it really any source for wonder or reason for scandal, that some of His successors have performed worse than poorly? But people don't make the connection.

Another cause of great scandal is whenever clerics are found guilty of financial impropriety. Bishops or priests who are caught with their hand in the till can reasonably plead that they are only following the example of the Church's first treasurer, Judas Iscariot, whose financial dishonesty rather pales into insignificance in comparison with the ultimate betrayal His greed for money led him into.

Human beings are very inconsistent. They are skeptical or suspicious of the Catholic Church's readiness to recognize that certain individuals have achieved a degree of perfection which seems utterly out of the reach of the ordinary person. They like to think, whether out of envy or just plain incredulity, that there must be some hidden flaws or weaknesses which have been covered up. They argue, quite reasonably on the basis of their own experience of fallen human life, that no one is perfect, or at least as perfect as that. Everybody is only "human" after all. The idea that it might be actually inhuman to be less than perfect would come as a considerable shock to them. So-called saints appear unreal. If the Catholic Church is not guilty of chicanery, then it probably has a convenient capacity for self-delusion.

What is so odd is that it is the very same people that throw up their hands in horror when prominent Catholics show that they do, indeed, have feet of clay who also get very dubious when the same Church recognizes that there are some—maybe comparatively very few—people who do get quite close to realizing in their lives the very goodness that Jesus Himself not only advocated but also promised would characterize those who were His true followers. In their earthly lives these saints cooperate with God, not just by doing His will but also by making Jesus Christ present in the world in a very visible way. One could argue that these men and women, these heroes and heroines of Christianity, are the best proof of all of its truth. For surely if we cannot find comparable figures of quite this stature in other religions or philosophies of life—as I have already claimed—then those beliefs which make them behave as they do are surely very well worth taking seriously. We have already seen how Jesus intended to go on being present through His chosen people, the Spirit-filled Church, rather than through a book or body of teachings, although both these are the precious possessions of the same Church. Well, it is through the most important members of this Church that He makes Himself most concretely and powerfully present in the world. And of all these saints none can compete with His mother, Mary.

Of all the human cooperators that God has employed, no one comes near to her in significance. She is crucial to the realization of the Incarnation. The human race's fate depended on the answer she gave to God. As I have already pointed out, her active role doesn't cease there. After all, God might have asked her simply to be the biological channel through which His Word could enter this world as a human being; He might have told her that once she had given birth to Jesus, her role would then come to an end. The baby would be spirited away somewhere, and Mary would be in the position of a mother who gives away her baby at birth to be looked after by a foster mother or orphanage. But in fact, of course, God did nothing of the sort. He intended Mary not merely to be the natural mother but the real mother who looks after her baby and brings Him up, albeit with the help of Joseph, who was the foster father.

When we start reflecting on the implications of this, we begin to realize just how important Mary was. The gospel account makes it clear that Jesus had to grow up and mature to manhood like any other baby. He definitely wasn't an adult in the disguise of a baby! He was a real, though unique baby. Just as He wasn't less human but more human than any other human being who has ever lived, so too He wasn't a quasi-baby; He was a real baby, a helpless baby dependent on His mother for His food and care. If Mary didn't look after Him, then He suffered like any other baby. Like all babies He became a toddler, a child, and then an adolescent before finally becoming at last an adult.

As His mother in the fullest sense of the word, Jesus no doubt got His looks from her and her family alone, since Joseph was not His birth father. We hear from one of the gospel accounts that His neighbors in His hometown, Nazareth, referred to Him as the son of Mary—as though it was recognized somehow that Joseph was not His true father. Just as we all owe an enormous amount, for better or worse, to our parents, to those who brought us up, so too we can surely say that in His humanity Jesus owed a very great deal indeed to Mary, and to a lesser extent, to Joseph too. Even when He reached manhood, Jesus apparently stayed at home with His family for a number of years before beginning the mission on which He had been sent by His Father to accomplish in this world.

Now it might be objected that if Mary is so important, why doesn't the New Testament say more about her? To that three points can be made. First, the New Testament writers were inevitably and rightly concerned with communicating what they knew about Jesus Christ. No one else, not even His mother, must be allowed to take too central a place on the stage. Second, we are told that when Mary received her extraordinary message from God, she "pondered" on what she had learned. And in this respect, as in many others, she is the model not only for the individual Christian but for the Church as a whole. For the Church, like any of her members, must reflect on what has been revealed to her. And so, like Mary, the Church "pondered" the role of Mary in the succeeding centuries, particularly after the Church had grappled successfully with the question of the identity of Jesus Christ, man but also God, God but also man. This is that process of development at which we have already looked. Then third, the New Testament evidence is rather more substantial than I have indicated. For while Mary may fade into the background after her initial appearance center-stage at the conception and birth of Jesus, it is remarkable how she keeps reappearing at key moments in the story.

When Jesus works His first miracle, it is at her request. As I have already commented, it is a rather strange miracle, indeed a rather shocking miracle one would have thought for those who read the Gospels in too literal and simplistic a way. Like any literature, the writings of the Bible have to be read with imagination and awareness of context. It is only, for example, when we have finished a novel that earlier episodes may make sense. A good detective writer leaves clues for the reader, including misleading clues sometimes, to maintain the suspense and to hold the reader's interest. Well, the Gospels aren't detective stories but they are full of clues. A key moment when Jesus begins His public mission is when He stands up in the synagogue on the Sabbath and proceeds to read from one of the Old Testament prophets. Just as in Christian churches, so in Jewish synagogues there were people appointed to read the readings for the particular day. In Jesus' case, He doesn't Himself choose from where the reading was to come. It is handed to Him and when He opens it He finds it is the book of Isaiah, who more than any other of the Old Testament prophets mysteriously predicted the Messiah who was to come, a Messiah who looked remarkably like Jesus Himself as events unfolded. It seems as though Jesus Himself found the passage He wanted to read rather than its being chosen for Him. But either way, the passage was about the Spirit being given to the prophet to announce the good news that God is going to liberate His people. Jesus thereupon sits down and preaches to them that the text was actually now being fulfilled as they listened to Him. This is an example of a very obvious clue, which only the most obtuse could miss.

Very often, then, the significance of an action or saying in the Gospels depends upon the background of the Jewish scriptures. Sometimes the real meaning can only become clear in the light of later events. In the case of the miracle at the wedding reception in Cana, Mary remarks to Jesus that the wine has run out. Addressing His mother very strangely as "woman," He understands her to be saying that He should do something about it, and replies that it is not His business since His "hour has not come yet." Ignoring His objection, Mary tells the staff to do whatever He tells them, whereupon He tells them to fill some water jars with water which then turns into wine. Now it is unthinkable that Jesus would have insulted His mother by rudely addressing her as "woman" because He was angry with her for disturbing Him by her remark. Clearly, the address is intended in some mysteriously formal sense. Saint Paul realized that Jesus was the new Man, the new Adam who had come to restore what the first man Adam had lost. By the second century the Christian consciousness has taken in the fact that Mary is the new Eve, the new mother of the redeemed human race.

But what about this "hour" that Jesus says has not yet come? Again, later Christian reflection connected this "hour" with Jesus' crucifixion when He entrusted His mother, who was there, to John, the disciple closest to Him, with the words, "Behold, your mother" (John 19:27). It was understood that just as an injunction given to the head apostle Peter was intended for all the apostles, so too John here, representing the principle of love rather than faith or authority, stood for the whole Church in a different, non-hierarchical way. In other words, now that His final hour has come, so too His mother's hour has come, as she is now to be the Mother of the Church, able to bring the requests of the members of the Church before the risen Jesus in heaven.

Finally, when the Church is fully established by the Holy Spirit at Pentecost, once again we find Mary there praying along with the apostles. In spite of what may seem the comparative silence about Mary in the Gospels, the fact is she is there at the key moments. Above all she is the one who gives birth to Jesus and who is also there at His death suffering with Him, sharing as it were in His crucifixion. But, hugely important and significant as Mary is, it would be quite wrong to think that she was some kind of superwoman through her own merits. Like all of us, she was called to cooperate and she could, like Eve, have failed. But, like all of us again, there is nothing she can do apart from what she is endowed with by her creator. If we can make free choices, it is because we have been given free will. But our failures to make the right choices are not by any means all our fault, as we have been handicapped by that innate tendency to sin which is built into us and which is called original sin. Similarly, in order to make the right choices, particularly assent to the Incarnation, Mary had to be given a special immunity from this tendency, as she was after all only human like us. In order decisively to break the cycle of sin and enable His Word to enter this world, God had to give her immunity from that fatal orientation which so frustrates us despite all our good intentions and all our partial successes. Mary, then, was specially privileged, so the great significance she has for Catholics (and naturally Orthodox) is by no means the result entirely of her own efforts. She certainly did fully cooperate with God who had not taken away her free will when God especially endowed her with what is called in theological parlance "grace," which means God's special favor or help. So she could have refused in principle to do what was asked of her, but in practice she was immeasurably aided by being effectively put back into the situation of Eve before she succumbed to evil. This is all that is meant by the doctrine of "the Immaculate Conception": Mary was conceived without that compulsive leaning toward sin which is the lot of the disinherited human race descended from the "ruined" Adam and Eve, who threw away their endowment by suicidally asserting themselves in preference to God. In other words, Mary was conceived not as some sort of superhuman person, but merely as a normal, rather than abnormal, human being, equipped with the properly functioning human nature God had originally given to human beings, rather than with the disoriented nature that remained of the original inheritance which Adam and Eve were meant to pass on to their descendants.

There is another reason why Mary needed to be favored in this very special way. For, after all, she herself had to conceive and give birth to the God-man, the Jesus who was sinlessly perfect. It would surely be hard to imagine how He could be born of a sinful woman, with a fallen human nature, inevitably self-regarding and self-assertive—however good and holy she might be—as opposed to being oriented toward God and therefore also oriented toward human fulfillment and happiness. I suppose that if one thinks of Mary as just a more or less passive biological instrument whom God simply takes over and uses entirely as He pleases, then perhaps it is not so difficult to imagine a sinlessly perfect Jesus simply passing through her body as a convenience, but a body that had really little to do with Him except in a purely physical sense. If, on the other hand, we take Mary's motherhood seriously—as the gospel accounts surely suggest we should—then it is important in what kind of a woman's womb Jesus was conceived and existed for nine months, what kind of a woman gave Him her milk, what kind of a woman first held and cuddled Him in her arms. If we are really going to take Jesus' humanity seriously, then we really have no option but to take very seriously what sort of a woman—if no man was involved—gave Him His physical existence and was the first and most intimate human contact He had. Of course, if we don't think that Jesus was really human at all but merely adopted a human disguise to carry out His mission and work in this world, then no doubt there isn't any problem. Similarly, if we don't think that Jesus was really God but just an extraordinary man filled with the spirit of God as no other human being ever has been, then also there is no particular—or at least not nearly the same—reason to bother too much about what kind of a woman was His mother.

We still need to be clear how, as well as why, Mary was immune from original sin. This privileged exemption she owed completely to her Son. God did not make a special exception in her case in the sense of restoring her to original innocence separately from Christ. She, like us, was totally dependent on the Incarnation, death, and Resurrection of Jesus. Without His saving mission Mary could not have been privileged as she was. God's plan for the human race did not allow any exceptions to what only Jesus could do. The fact that she was saved from the moment of her conception retroactively by what Jesus was to accomplish puts her in a very special place. But she, like everyone else, could only be saved by Jesus. So from that point of view there is no difference between Mary and the rest of us.

If we turn to the way in which Jesus was conceived, we can see that both the divine and the human sides of His person were, so to speak, represented. That is to say, there was no human father involved, but God as Holy Spirit took the initiative as opposed to a man. On the other hand, it was a real woman who took part in the "intercourse" as a result of which Jesus was conceived. Once again, we could say that, provided we really do believe in the Incarnation, then this is practically a doctrine we could have guessed for ourselves. It was a quite unique conception, and therefore its cause also had to be quite unique, for the baby who was conceived and born was both divine and human. Jesus was a member of the human race, with a family tree, with relations—He wasn't created in heaven as a human being, with some special human nature devised by God quite separately from the rest of the human race. But, on the other hand, He owed His human existence entirely to God's initiative. Both in His divinity and His humanity He has only God as Father.

Now there are Christians who are prepared to accept the truth and even necessity of the virginal conception, but who find it very hard to comprehend why the tradition that goes back to the earliest times calls Mary "ever-virgin." Surely once her job was completed, Mary and Joseph could have normal marital relations. The idea that they never had sex seems to fly in the face of common sense and suggests some strangely morbid hang-up on the part of the early Church. Well, certainly, if one sees Mary as just graciously performing a biological role at God's request, then, no doubt there is no reason why she and Joseph could not just live ordinary married lives. But if Mary was a great deal more than a merely passive instrument, then surely the situation begins to look rather different.

After all, Mary was in a very real sense already "married." To have married Joseph would have been tantamount to adultery. Not only had she submitted her body to God's "desire," but she had given her heart as well not to another man but to her divine "lover." To be plain, Mary was in love with "somebody" else; she couldn't give Joseph her heart, the exclusive kind of love we associate with marriage. The gospel account calls her "full of grace," and grace as we have seen means God's love directed at us, supporting us. So to be "full of grace" means literally to be full of this love, inundated with it. Flooded with God's love, Mary could only respond with a heart full of love for God. Human beings were created to love God; the tragedy of Adam and Eve was loving themselves more than God. The whole point of the picturesque story at the beginning of the Bible is to express the profound truth—which Jesus announces again—that self-love leads to unhappiness and unfulfillment, whereas love of God leads to happiness and fulfillment.

I said that Jesus had a family tree, but He also started a quite different, a quite new, family tree. The woman who is at the head of this new family tree is His mother Mary, but the father of this tree is God, God as Holy Spirit. Only God can be the Father of this new family which owes its existence to the Holy Spirit—and to Mary, the spiritual "wife" of the Spirit. This family, of course, is the new creation, the new People of God, the Church, with Christ, who comes from heaven, as opposed to Adam, who is created from the earth, as its Head. But the Word of God can only come down to join the human race because there is a woman who is so filled with God's Spirit that she can also be filled, impregnated with God's Word. And as the human Jesus is conceived by the action of the Spirit, so the members of the new creation are born into the Church through the Holy Spirit. Mary is the mother of this Church, which, like Mary, listens to God's voice and conceives her spiritual children because she is empowered by the Spirit to do so.

Finally, we come to the question of the end of Mary's earthly life. We speak about the "holy places," meaning the places traditionally associated with Christ, including where He was buried. Over the centuries they have been constantly visited by pilgrims. To a much lesser extent, Rome, the capital of the Roman Empire, where both Saint Peter and Saint Paul were martyred, has also been considered a special place for pilgrimage. The odd thing is that there is no place where Mary is traditionally held to have been buried. This is surely very singular indeed. After Jesus there was no more important person than Mary, and yet she seems just mysteriously to disappear from view.

The Catholic (and Orthodox) understanding is that this mysterious fact can be very easily explained. It would hardly have been fitting that the body of the woman who conceived, who bore Jesus, out of whose flesh He came, should have been allowed by God to molder away in the earth. That body was uniquely precious, as was the person whose body it was. Just as she was uniquely privileged above other human beings, so it was only appropriate that when her human life ended, she should enjoy a uniquely privileged end. Whether in fact she died an ordinary death is not recorded in the Christian tradition. What, though, is believed and taught as a doctrine by the Catholic Church is that she was fittingly singled out to share in a very special way in her son's Resurrection by herself being raised at the end of her life immediately into heaven, not just her soul but her body, too. This is what is meant by the doctrine of the "Assumption," or what in the Orthodox Church is called the "Dormition" or falling asleep. It was the resurrection of the whole person, no different from the eventual resurrection of every human person who enters the condition and state of heaven, only different in its mode and immediacy. Otherwise Mary's Assumption only anticipates the resurrection of all who are saved by Christ.

CHAPTER 14

THE CHURCH'S BODY LANGUAGE

As bodily beings, we express ourselves through our bodies as well as through our words, whether oral or in writing. Our thoughts and feelings emerge and communicate themselves to others by what is called our "body language." When we meet somebody for the first time, the impression we get of him or her comes perhaps as much from what we see as from what we hear. This is hardly surprising in view of the fact that our bodies are not instruments somehow external to us, which we merely use, but are an integral part of what constitutes us as human beings. A look on someone's face, a smile, a glare, may make words redundant and be far more expressive than any words. Indeed, sometimes a physical gesture may make redundant words far more eloquent than anything that can be said. In other words, the signals we send out emanate as much from our body language as from our verbal language. In fact, at moments of particular intensity, we may naturally prefer to send out a physical sign rather than putting anything in words. For there are times when words are not just hard to find but seem completely inadequate. The first moment that two lovers hold hands or kiss is going to be a far more expressive moment than any previous verbal communications.

The reader may wonder what all this has to do with what has preceded. Its relevance is this: having talked so much about the Church and about how one cannot understand what Catholicism is all about without understanding its idea of the Church—the question of how one becomes a member of this Church, and why one does join the Church in this particular way, suggests itself as the next subject that has to be looked at. But before we consider what

Baptism is and how and why it is the means by which one enters the Church, we need to consider, in a more general way, what is meant by the sacraments, of which Baptism is one.

I have been talking about signals or signs, and one or two distinctions need to be made. There are some signs which are quite arbitrary. If I belong to a secret society, there may be a particular handshake or a particular badge of some sort which will reveal me as a member of the society, but the sign will only be recognizable to other members of the society or those who happen to be in the know. To anyone else the sign will mean nothing, because there is nothing about the sign that can possibly carry any meaningful associations. There are, however, some signs which are pictorially expressive and easily intelligible, such as certain road signs, for instance, which may be used quite meaningfully in different countries with different languages.

There are also signs which not only indicate something which is obvious to everyone, but actually express, embody, realize that which they signify. I am thinking of something like a kiss: unless the person kissing is a Judas who means the opposite of that which it signifies, a kiss both denotes affection and love *and* is a concrete expression of this affection and love. It not only sends out a recognizable signal; it also effects that which it signifies. We would think it very odd if somebody, a husband say, were to suggest to his wife that in the future, for hygienic reasons, they should indicate their affection for each other by, for example, waving a handkerchief. If his wife agreed to this novel sign, then the sign would work at the level of conveying the existence of the feeling of affection. What such a sign would not and could not do would be to serve as an effective way not just of indicating but of expressing in the sense of *enacting* the feeling of affection. For when somebody sincerely kisses another person, they are doing a great deal more than announcing to that person and anyone else who happens to be there that there exists in them a feeling of affection or love for the other person. They are not merely signifying their feeling of love, they are actually exercising the emotion by putting it into practice by, quite simply, loving.

With, then, a sign like a kiss, we have three elements in the body language: we have the act of signifying, we have a signification which is immediately recognizable to anyone, *and* we have the third concrete element of enactment. That is to say, the body language not only says something that everybody understands, it actually does that which it says. In the case of the Church, we call the equivalent of such body language the "sacraments." Like human beings, like the community made up of these individuals, the Church and her members individually not only employ verbal language but also body language. And the sacraments constitute the most important and fundamental part of this body language. The Church announces and informs the world about Jesus Christ; she makes her message known orally, as well as in writing, above all in the Bible. She also expresses herself through actions, actions which not only signify what the Church intends to say, but furthermore bring about, effect, and realize in the concrete that which is meant. Of course, these actions are also accompanied by words, just as kisses by themselves, without any words indicating feeling, would suggest lust rather than love.

As I have said, human beings have a bodily as well as a mental life, although the two are closely intertwined and inseparable from each other. Together, they make up the reality we call a human being. Well, the individual human beings who constitute the Church do not leave behind their bodies when it comes to their membership in the new liberated human race or community which is the Church. All together, indeed, they make up what the Church calls the one Body of Christ. This single body is made up of many separate bodies, just as the human race is. And so, like its individual members, the whole Church also has its body, as well as verbal language, not that the two can ever really be separated from each, any more than human bodies and minds exist on two quite separate plains.

What, then, the Church says, she also signifies through various actions. Some of these actions or signs only operate like the secret handshake or token, others are more like those graphic traffic signs which indicate something easily recognizable and understandable. There is also a third kind of body or sign language the Church employs which, like a kiss, actually and concretely effects, realizes, and brings about that which it recognizably signifies. This is what is meant by a sacrament as opposed to a "sacramental." Both words come from a Latin word meaning "sacred." But a sacramental doesn't actually "do" anything. It is like the second sign: it is pretty obvious what it intends to signify, yet it doesn't realize that which it indicates so clearly. It is like the kind of pictorial road sign that can be used in different countries with different languages and carry a common meaning evident to everyone precisely because it is a graphic, rather than written, sign. It stands in contrast to an entirely arbitrary road sign, like painting part of the road green to indicate, say, a bus route, which doesn't speak for itself but can only have meaning to the inhabitants of that particular country. Somebody who knew nothing about the Catholic Church could hardly be expected to understand that purple ecclesiastical clothing denotes a bishop, since there is no particular or obvious reason why a bishop should wear purple as opposed to the white dress of the pope. The use of water to symbolize purification or oil to represent healing should not be so esoteric to an outsider, who could not be expected to appreciate the significance of making the Sign of the Cross unless he knew about the Christian understanding of the crucifixion of Jesus Christ.

A sacrament, on the other hand, means much more than these. Like a hug or a kiss, a sacrament not only sends a clear signal, it also embodies or enacts what it signifies. And the analogy with a bodily sign like a hug or a kiss is very appropriate, since the sacraments also both signify and are the concrete expression of love, but in this case the love of God. Now, there are people who regard themselves as Christians but have a limited view of sacraments. To them, being a Christian is, more or less, an entirely spiritual matter; it is a matter of faith, of prayer, and of trying to live a Christian life, with the Bible as one's guide. But, as we have seen, this opposition or separation of the spiritual from the physical is not true to human life as we experience it. We are embodied spiritual beings: we have minds but we also have bodies which affect our mental lives and through and in which we feel and think. There would be something very strange, indeed inhuman, about someone who couldn't see the point of physically expressing emotions. To restrict oneself to an inner life without reference to one's body would be to restrict life itself. We call such a person inhibited or reserved in the extreme. We recognize there is something limited, not quite human about him.

Another point needs to be made here about the purpose of such body language as hugging and kissing. It is not just that such physical behavior is the natural and obvious way of showing one's feelings, not just that it gives vent to our feelings; there is a further consideration that is important. A husband who is very undemonstrative in showing affection to his wife and children not only arouses in them an insecurity about whether he really loves them, not only fails to give proper expression to his love, but, in addition, he is in danger of damaging, diminishing, or even losing his love for them (not to mention their love for him). No one with the slightest horticultural sense puts a plant into his garden and expects it to flourish, or even survive, without continuing care. It would be a foolish gardener who thought that it was enough to plant it in the right sort of place and soil and with the appropriate kind of fertilizer, water it once, and then let nature take its course—which would very likely be to the detriment of the plant.

Exactly the same is true about the body language we employ to express affection and love. Without a handshake (or the equivalent bodily sign appropriate to the culture), there is something missing in a merely verbal greeting. Obviously, social customs vary, but instinctively we feel that something more than words is required, particularly on a first introduction. We feel, in fact, the need to use our bodies as well as our voices. Ascending the scale, the same is true of the hug, the kiss, linking arms, and holding hands. Again, cultures vary, but universally there is recognition of the human need to give physical expression to emotions and feelings. On the most intimate of all levels, marital love demands sexual intercourse. In all of these situations, we are not only talking about what seems appropriate and natural; we are also alluding to the spontaneous way in which we forge, sustain, and build up our relationships with other people. Like the gardener who thinks that the plant will inevitably grow without further attention provided it receives the proper treatment when it is planted, the abnormally reserved and undemonstrative husband and father will find that love requires continual fostering, if only to survive, let alone grow. It would be very odd if he were to say to his wife that he couldn't understand why she should want physical expressions of his love when it was so evident that he loved her from all his other actions. Was it not enough that he had in the past, at the beginning of their marriage, displayed his love in the usual physical ways? Why was it necessary to go on repeating signs when the reality of his love lay before her in the ways he provided for the family, helped her in the house more than most husbands, looked after the garden, and so on. Might not his wife be provoked into retorting that she would really prefer some other concrete demonstrations of his love: an occasional hug or kiss, for example, would be far preferable to all his arduous activities in the garden. And surely his wife's frustration would extend beyond her disappointment at the lack of the sort of body language that normally accompanies sentiments which she might have no reason at all to doubt. What would also be missing, apart from the immediate gratification of her own bodily needs, would be the ongoing development and growth of their relationship. For relationships, like life itself, as we have already seen, depend on their development, otherwise they don't just remain static, but decline. If the climber clings to his precarious foothold rather than continuing his ascent up the mountain, he is likely to find that, eventually, his foothold gives way and he falls back, perhaps disastrously. Not to go on doesn't at all mean that one will stay where one is. And so, continuing body language has to accompany a relationship as it develops; it is by no means simply restricted to the signs that may well be appropriate signals to signify inner states of feeling at the beginning of a relationship. If we are to continue to love in new situations and new circumstances, if we want our love to increase rather than decrease, then we have to continue to express our love in and through the appropriate body language. To go on loving is to go on kissing, not to call it a day once the relationship has been established.

In the same way, sacraments, and also sacramentals, build up and nourish the Christian's relationship with Christ and His life in the Church. It is true that some sacraments are not repeated but others are, particularly that sacrament which gives the Christian the equivalent of the food and drink without which human life cannot exist. That sacrament not only provides the necessary sustenance, but it also, like the kiss or the hug, contributes to, and enhances the growth of, the Christian's relationship with Christ and His Church. We want to go on touching in the appropriate manner those we like or love; so, too, the Christian wants to go on touching Christ through His sacramental Body and Blood. But we must postpone our discussion of that. In the meantime, there are two further points to be made before we end this consideration of what I have called the body language of the Church.

First, this body language which accompanies, and indeed is an integral part of, the Christian life as it is of human life is the key to understanding why Catholic (and, needless to say, Orthodox) churches seem so different from Protestant churches. In the latter, the emphasis, to a greater or lesser extent, is on words, that is to say, on prayers, readings, hymns, and sermons. In the former kind of churches, in addition to all these words, there is a great deal of body language involved in the celebration of the sacraments and the use of sacramentals. Thus Catholics don't simply walk into church and sit down. They cross themselves with holy water as they enter. They bow or genuflect to the tabernacle where the bread consecrated at the Eucharist is kept and where, therefore, they believe Jesus Christ is sacramentally present. Similar bodily movements accompany the celebration of the Eucharist. Before leaving the church, the Catholic is quite likely to kneel before a statue of Jesus or Mary or another saint, having lit a candle. Obviously, the more sacramental a Protestant church is, the more movement, the more body language there is likely to be. But there will never be anything like the kind of physical activity that occurs in a Catholic church thanks to the preeminent place given to the sacraments and the easy familiarity with sacramentals. The contrast is between a building made primarily for the saying and singing of words and a building where words are accompanied by, and reflected in, the body language.

Second, before we look at the different individual sacraments, we need to remember there is another sacrament without which none of the seven traditional sacraments could exist, and that is the Church herself, which is the fundamental or, as it were, original sacrament. We have seen that, like a kiss, a sacrament is a sign which not only signifies but which also brings about and makes concrete that which it signifies. And the same is clearly true of the Church which is *the* paramount sign of Christ in the world and which is a sign that really does make Christ present, in a whole variety of ways. In being *the* sign of Christ which makes all the other signs possible, the Church is the sign of the liberating mission of Christ through the agency of the Spirit, the effective or instrumental sign of the sharing in the divine life which that mission makes possible and of the new human unity that results from that sharing.

Perhaps the most obviously visible way in which the Church herself is *the* instrumental sign is in the buildings where the Church's mission statement is publicly announced, especially through its "services." Since the Church can exist, as it did in the early days, without its own buildings because the Church is not a material building but a building made up of the human beings who make up the community or people of Christ, the Church is ultimately an effective sign in so far as its members individually and corporately are effective signs of Christ. For to be an effective sign of Christ is to be somebody who both indicates Christ and is also the instrument who makes Christ's presence a concrete kind of reality.

CHAPTER 15

TAKING THE PLUNGE

We have seen how becoming a Christian means joining the Church, not just as a sort of pragmatic consequence of faith and wanting to share and express that belief with others, but as an integral and necessary part of becoming a Christian. So how do we join the Church?

We might very easily suppose that it would be like, say, being naturalized as a citizen of a country. Presumably, some affirmation of adherence and assent to that country's constitution, perhaps in the form of a sworn oath of loyalty, would be required. We might also guess that some symbolic ceremony would accompany the verbal act to bring out the solemnity of the occasion. Perhaps the person would be asked to kiss the crucifix, for example, rather like one might have to salute the flag of the country of which one wished to become a citizen. Now there are many believers in Christ who see it very much like that. For them, Baptism is merely a symbolic act which simply externalizes and solemnizes an essentially internal act, the act of believing, although with the added dimension of expressing in public one's decision to join the visible community of believers.

This, however, is not the Catholic understanding of Baptism, which involves significantly more than this. The Catholic view of Baptism is that it is not just a sacramental but a sacrament, and, as we have seen, a sacrament is not only a sign which signifies but a sign which effects or realizes that which it signifies. So Baptism is not only an external sign of internal faith, as well as a visible entry into the community of faith, but it is actually at one and the same time the instrument of our escape from the imprisonment of sin and of our finding freedom in the community of liberation, the new People of God. In other words, Baptism is the concrete means by which we are both rescued from ourselves by Christ and adopted into his family.

The word "baptize" comes from a Greek word meaning plunge in water. How, it may be asked, can a physical act like that, involving a material substance, have anything to do with spiritual regeneration? Before attempting to answer this question, though, we do need to note that the sacrament of Baptism involves more than immersion in water. As in the other sacraments, there is a prayer to the Holy Spirit, in this case to empower the water to give the new spiritual birth which is Baptism. And, at the moment of immersion or plunging in water, the person performing the sacrament accompanies his action by the words, "I baptize you in the name of the Father and of the Son and of the Holy Spirit." There is, therefore, a vital verbal element, as well as the material and physical elements.

But even so, the claim is that physical water is somehow spiritualized and that the act of Baptism actually changes, indeed drastically transforms, the person who is baptized. We must, therefore, look at what kind of change is envisaged in the sacraments, particularly the Eucharist, when no apparent physical change, in fact, takes place.

In a scientific age we naturally tend to think of changes, especially where material objects are involved, as being necessarily physical. To plunge somebody in water and then to pronounce that that person has been transformed spiritually by the action suggests to the modern mind that the water and the plunging must be purely symbolic, as if they could not possibly have anything to do with an inner change in the person. What, rather, must be important are the person's own feelings and intentions which are merely expressed, or at best reinforced, by the baptismal sign. When it comes to the baptism of babies, who are not even conscious of what is happening to them, even Catholics may well suppose that nothing really happens to the baby at all. What must surely count is the attitude of the parents (and godparents) to the ceremony, which must really be about what they wish to express and intend. Yet the Church pronounces that the baby *has* undergone a change, *has* acquired a new birth, a new identity, and not merely figuratively. The conclusion must be that either the Church cannot be speaking literally or it is talking prescientific magical nonsense. But the Catholic Church is categorical that the sacraments are not magic—that is, they do not manipulate people against their will. Instead, the sacraments require human cooperation; the initiative is divine, but the response has to be human. So where does that leave us?

It leaves us, or takes us back to, the question of change. For by no means are all changes in human life material or physical. This is so even when these elements are involved and even when they are integral to the process of change. For instance, an immigrant to a country where achieving citizenship requires not only an oath of loyalty but saluting the flag, say, does undergo a hugely important change of identity on receiving his new nationality—and yet, although the necessary ceremony of naturalization includes the physical and material elements of saluting the flag, no *physical* change whatsoever takes place in the naturalized person. Or, to take another example, a mother may bake two sponge cakes for her children, which are identical in their ingredients and consequently in how they look and taste. One of these cakes she designates, however, as a birthday cake by virtue of sticking the requisite number of candles in it. She may also enclose the cake with fancy wrapping, but when it comes to the blowing out of the candles and the cutting of the cake, the birthday cake has not experienced any material change. If the child, whose birthday it is, later pronounces that the other iced sponge cake which is eaten on a subsequent occasion doesn't taste nearly as good, it would be assumed the child was speaking with rhetorical hyperbole to show his pleasure and thanks for the birthday party. For, of course, the second cake doesn't taste any different or better than the first birthday cake. They are identical in appearance and taste. Nevertheless, one is the birthday cake and the other is not. One has a special significance which the other doesn't have. Everyone at the birthday party is expected to have a slice of the birthday cake. Not to do so would be to distance oneself from the birthday party, to refuse to enter into the occasion, even to cause offense. It wouldn't at all matter if the same person later also refused a slice of the second, identical cake. Indeed, there would be no expectation that he or she would want a piece.

The fact is that things, as well as people, can be changed, indeed transformed, without any material or physical alteration at all taking place. A man who becomes a father for the first time may undergo a huge change of personality, but, unlike his wife, nothing remotely physical has happened to him. There is no reason, then, why analogous changes may not take place in the spiritual sphere. On the contrary, there is every reason to suppose that real spiritual transformations will not be reflected in any physical change. That is not to say that what happens spiritually may not be externally accompanied by physical actions and material things.

What takes place in Baptism is effected by a combination of prayer and immersion in water. But the result is an entirely spiritual one. However, that doesn't mean that nothing really happens, any more than in the cases of the person who is naturalized and the man who becomes a father. They don't experience any physical permutation, but the change that does take place is certainly not imaginary. In these two instances, the persons concerned may well come to see the event as the most important in their life, perhaps the turning point in their life.

So what happens to a person who is baptized? The first thing to be aware of is that the other person, who is doing the baptizing, is only the agent of Jesus Christ. According to the Catholic understanding of the sacraments, it is always really Christ who makes the sacrament happen; whether it is a priest or any other human being who performs the sacrament, it is always as the agent or agents of Christ Himself. Without Jesus and the Holy Spirit, there couldn't be any sacraments anyway. It is Christ who instituted the sacraments—not necessarily explicitly in the Gospels, although that is true of five out of the seven sacraments, including, of course, Baptism. The sacraments are Christ doing things to human beings, acting always, of course, through the agency of His Church. But just as Christ needs the Spirit to be present in the Church and the individual believer, so too Christ performs the sacrament through the agency of the Spirit as well as through the human agent. For in every sacrament the Church prays to the Spirit to transform whatever is submitted to the Spirit's power. It is as though Christ can only act by sending His Father's and His love, which alone can change things like water into spiritual forces. For the Father is certainly not absent from any sacrament: He is there in the powerful love of Him and His Son, that divine love which is a person, the Holy Spirit.

The sacrament in question here is called after the word for plunging: for the immersion in water represents burial, a participation in Christ's death, and the rising out of the water stands for the resurrection which the baptized person now shares, becoming thereby a new person, or a Christian. But for all the symbolic nature of the action, this is no mere symbol. It is a sacrament which does something, which changes the person baptized into a different person. Water is indeed a potent symbol because it can stand for both destruction by drowning and flooding, but also for life, as without water nothing can live. And water which is used for cleaning also symbolizes purification. But the sacrament doesn't just consist of plunging in water; it also includes the prayer to the Spirit and the repetition of the words of Jesus telling the apostles to go out and baptize "in the name of the Father and of the Son and of the Holy Spirit" (Mt. 28:19). Without the verbal element, the material element of water couldn't do anything; it is only when the words encounter, as it were, the water, that one has the sacrament of Baptism.

When that is done, the person baptized, whether a baby or an adult, has become a naturalized citizen of God's nation. The old nation, which was limited to one nationality and one race, was liberated by God from slavery in Egypt by being brought safely across the waters of the Red Sea, and later across the water of the Jordan river to the safety of the promised land. The new nation is also liberated by means of water, but this time the liberation is not from political but from moral and spiritual slavery, the oppression that is sin. And again, not only is there a freeing from sin, but, as with the Jews, there is a promised land, the Church of Christ, in which the previously enslaved can enjoy a new life of freedom. The fact that a baby is not conscious of what is happening is of no more consequence than it would be if the baby were being naturalized along with the rest of his family and given a new nationality. In neither case is the baby consulted, and in either case the baby on growing up may later turn out to be an indifferent citizen or even repudiate his citizenship. The only difference is that the person who denies his acquired nationality may emigrate to another country and become a national of that country, the person who repudiates his Baptism cannot, however, actually be unbaptized any more than he can be "unborn." Baptism, which is a new spiritual birth, can no more be erased than birth itself, however much one may hate being alive; all one can do, in both cases, is to show dislike by one's behavior.

Again, of course, in both cases the naturalized baby, unlike the adult, has to learn later about his acquired new nationality. He has to find out after the event what sort of people he became a member of when he was too young to understand, what its laws and rules are, what it stands for, and so on. Conversely, the naturalized adult has a more or less clear understanding at the time of his naturalization.

The baptized person is smeared with oil blessed by a bishop to indicate that becoming a member of the Church is synonymous with being "invaded" by the Holy Spirit, whose power enables the Baptism. The love of the Father and the Son, the love which is God, takes hold of the baptized who is "adopted" as a member of the Trinitarian family, so to speak. The baptized Christian obviously is not a daughter or son of God the Father as the Son is. But still there is, as Jesus promised, a kind of adoption or affiliation whereby the Christian is brought into a new intimacy with God, which empowers him or her to relate to the Father as a child relates to his or her own parent. The transcendent all-powerful God can now be approached on an altogether new footing, thanks to sharing in the love which is the life of God who is love. The water used in the sacrament, signifying renewal, indicates this new life.

Like water, oil is a potent symbol, and never more so than in the modern world. Oil has always been used for cleaning, healing, and beautifying, as well as in cooking and eating. Not surprisingly, it is used in four of the sacraments. One of these is called "Confirmation," which, as the name suggests, is a sacrament of confirming or ratifying. It strengthens what is given in Baptism: the gift the Father and the Son send, which is their love or their Spirit, and the membership of the Church which this confers. What happened to the apostles at Pentecost now takes place for the baptized Christian: the Spirit is received in complete fullness. As with the apostles who suddenly discovered an extraordinary new strength to publicly profess Jesus Christ, so too the confirmed Christian is a full member of the Church, empowered to act and speak in her name. The confirmed Christian is now a "marked" person. We speak about somebody being a "marked" man or woman, meaning thereby that they have been specially noted, singled out from others, usually with a sinister intent. Well, the confirmed Christian, like the confirmed bachelor or the confirmed smoker or drinker or gambler, is somebody who has become an inveterate Christian, as it were, somebody who simply can't help being a Christian and recognizable as such by all. A confirmed Christian has been commissioned, entrusted with a mission to be a Christian, and the mark of this is the stamp or brand of the Holy Spirit.

However, there is still one further step that has to be taken by somebody who has "taken the plunge" in Baptism, and then or subsequently received the endorsement of that plunge in the sacrament of Confirmation. It is the reception of this third sacrament which completes one's full membership of the Church. It is the final part of the process which makes the Christian.

Greek word—are not more or less eucharistic than the original Last Supper. What happened then still happens.

Before we look at what is supposed to happen, we need to consider how an event can be both anticipated and recalled as though it were, in the first case, already taking place, and, in the second instance, how it can also somehow be happening when in fact it has already happened. An example of anticipation would be engagement, or "plighting one's troth," prior to the actual wedding. Since the Catholic Church regards the consent or agreement of a baptized man and woman to marry each other as the indispensable element of the sacrament of Marriage, there is a very real sense in which a formal engagement anticipates the actual marriage. If we stay with the example of marriage to offer an analogy for retrospective recollection, we could point to the way in which married couples can renew the vows they took at their wedding at a subsequent date. The wedding is now an event in the past, but retaking the same vows, as were taken previously, does in a very concrete way make the wedding happen again, as it were. It is not just the same as going out for dinner on one's wedding anniversary, or looking at the wedding photographs, or even watching the video of the wedding.

The event, which the Last Supper anticipated and which all subsequent reenactments of it recall, is the crucifixion, Christ's sacrifice of Himself for the sins of the world. On the night before His crucifixion, Jesus had in effect already offered Himself. The die was cast; there was no turning back; He was fully prepared mentally, after His agonized prayer to His Father in the Garden of Gethsemane, and He had accepted His destiny. He had as good as died, just as a formally engaged couple can be as good as married. For, at the Last Supper, Jesus did not simply announce to His apostles what was going to happen the next day and what it meant; He actually handed them the very body and blood that were to be sacrificed. Obviously, it was not the same physical person that was sitting at table with them. Neither the bread nor the wine that He gave them tasted like the flesh of the hands that handed them this very special food. They were hardly being invited to take part in a cannibalistic meal. Nevertheless, neither on this occasion nor on the previous occasion, to which we alluded earlier, when Jesus mysteriously told His listeners that if they wanted to be His adherents they would have to eat His Flesh and Blood, did

He give any indication that He was only speaking metaphorically. He didn't hasten to modify His extraordinary words by putting any sort of symbolic gloss on them. He didn't explain to His fellow diners at the Last Supper that He wanted them always to remember him and this night before He died by engaging in a similar sort of meal, when they would eat bread and drink wine as though, for example, they were eating and drinking His words, recorded for them in the memoirs that were to be written of His life.

Indeed, when you come to think of it, isn't it very odd, to say the least, that Jesus did not apparently make any attempt to appoint His official biographer or biographers from among the apostles or any other of His followers? This is something famous people regularly do, wanting to make sure that the true record, or the one they want, of their lives is published after their death. In the case of Jesus, it was surely all the more important that His teachings, His life, and His work were to be preserved after His death. But, as we have already seen, the picture completely changes once we realize that it was not in the first place to a book that Jesus intended to commit His legacy, but rather to a community, and a community to which He would always be present not only in spirit, but in much more concrete, personal ways. To begin with, it was not merely a matter of being vaguely present "in the spirit", as we say, but instead in *the* Spirit, and, moreover, not as a poor substitute for Himself but as *the* mode by which, or rather by whom, He could be immediately and personally present to any individual anywhere in the world and at any time. The presence was to be universal, but at the same time totally individual and personal. On top of this inner availability of Christ to the believer, there was always to be, in addition, another availability which was perfectly suited to corporeal human beings.

For at the Last Supper, and at every subsequent repetition of it, Jesus' followers are literally—although not carnally—promised the possibility of eating and drinking Jesus Christ. Now what we eat and drink not only sustains our bodies, enabling us to live, but it also affects the kind of bodies and health that we enjoy. If we drink a lot of alcohol, we may go red in the face, but equally we are told that red wine is good for the heart. Again, if we eat too many carbohydrates, we will get fat; if we eat healthy food full of vitamins, it will show on our faces. The deeply intimate and personal act of eating and drinking, whereby we introduce substances into our bodies, enables our bodies to survive, as well as determines what kind of bodies we will have. By placing a meal, then, at the center of His Church's life, Jesus was making a very eloquent point. It was not to be enough that His followers should read about Him and pray to Him; they were certainly to do that but they were also to have *Him* as their very food and drink. And just as with ordinary food, this spiritual nourishment would both enable them to live spiritually and would color and shape the nature of this spiritual life. They were to "live on" Christ, as somebody might live on bread and water, and their diet would be reflected in their lives—they would look like Christ. This regimen was to form their spiritual constitutions, just as material food and drink affect the way our bodies look and perform.

Once again, it is necessary to insist that there is not a stark alternative: the bread and wine of the Last Supper are not *either* simply symbolic of Christ's body and blood *or* literally His Body and Blood in the physical sense. Somebody or something, as we have seen, can change its identity without any physical change at all, but the change can still be real and substantial and not only token. A profound change with far-reaching implications takes place when somebody changes his nationality. When a newborn baby is given a name by its parents, the baby ceases to be just "he" or "she": it is now possible to refer to the baby by a name. In a very real sense the baby now becomes an identifiable person. But suppose those parents were unable to agree or make up their minds on a name; then the baby would be like a stateless person without a passport. Such a person doesn't in a sense "exist"; no state recognizes his existence. If the baby grows up without any name, or at least without any fixed name, then the growing child is going to have big problems. "He" or "she" will, for instance, go to school without an identity.

Well, when the Last Supper is repeated in the Eucharist, the bread and wine are called something different; so in our analogy the baby becomes "John," and so the bread and wine become the person of Christ. No physical change at all takes place in either case, but something momentous of a permanent nature happens. The baby is given an identity, the bread and wine, rather like the person who becomes a naturalized citizen of a foreign country, are, as it were, given a new identity. But, of course, analogies can never be pressed too hard. The bread and wine, over which certain prayers and words have been said, can't later on change this new identity. The new reality is more than a change which can be changed again, like a name or a nationality, which can be altered by deed-poll or naturalization. As we saw when talking about the "body language" of the Church, there are all sorts of different kinds of change. The change we are talking about in the Eucharist is a "sacramental" change whereby something takes on a new spiritual reality or significance. Because the Eucharistic food and drink are obviously not physical flesh—they look, smell, and taste exactly the same as they were before the Spirit was asked to transform them and before they were "named" as Christ's Body and Blood—does not mean that they haven't "really" changed at all. They have changed and undergone a real transformation, even though our senses can't detect any change. You can't tell by looking at a man that he is a father or what nationality he is or whether he is a politician or a scientist or an artist. Reality is not like that, except when we are talking about things in a purely physical way. When a sovereign is crowned or a president sworn in, that person becomes a king or queen or president, and remains so until he or she abdicates or resigns or reaches the end of the term of office. But we don't look for that person to change the color of his or her hair or skin or to get suddenly fat or thin, just because he or she has become a head of state. Well, it would be just as absurd and ridiculous to expect any such change in the Eucharist. In both cases, such an expectation would betray a naively literal mind.

We need now to pursue this line of argument in order to understand how the Eucharistic food is sacrificial food, in what sense the Christian is supposed to be partaking of what has been sacrificially slain. The original chosen people offered up two kinds of sacrifice: holocausts in which the entire animal was offered to God, and "peace offerings" in which only a choice part of the victim was offered to God, while the remainder provided a banquet for the offerer and his friends and family. In the latter kind of sacrifice, the sharing of the animal by God and human beings established a sort of communion between them. In what sense can the Eucharist be a sacrifice when no killing takes place? And how can Catholics identify the Eucharist with the sacrifice which took place on the Cross? After all, Jesus' recorded words only speak about a memorial—"Do this in remembrance of me" (Lk. 22:19).

It all depends on what one means by memory. Remembering somebody or something may be a quite inert sort of act: "Oh yes, I remember now." A past or absent person or event or thing comes back to the mind, but remains only a memory, more or less dim. However, suppose somebody shows one a photograph of a dead friend which one has never seen before, and suppose the photograph is an unusually good one and catches the dead friend's face or expression in a strikingly distinctive way—in that case, there is a very real sense in which the dead person comes back to life. It is as if he suddenly appears from the dead. Certainly memory is involved, but in this sort of instance somebody who belongs to the past, so to speak, suddenly becomes vividly present again. Something actually happens. Or it may be, to change the example, that a detective investigating a crime suddenly remembers something that was said by a witness or the look on somebody's face—with the flash of memory something clicks in his mind and what's remembered takes on a completely new significance. It is as if the words are heard for the first time, the look seen for the first time. The memory is far more vivid than the original experience; what is in the past enters the present more forcibly than it did in the past.

What impression, in fact, did the Last Supper have on the apostles at the time? The crucifixion and Resurrection had not yet happened, so inevitably the significance of what Jesus was doing must have been more or less lost on them. It was only in the light of future events that the Last Supper's meaning fully dawned on them. When, therefore, the first Eucharists were celebrated, there must have been a real sense in which the meal was invested with a significance which the Last Supper could not have had. The past event was now lighted up by subsequent developments. The Last Supper became more real and vivid in the memory of the Church than it had been for those who had actually participated in it.

Memory, then, can be as dynamic as it can be inert. And when Jesus instructed His Church to do what He had done "in memory" of Him, this doesn't at all have to imply the kind of memorial that simply calls to mind what can no longer be experienced, what is now buried in the past. When the Jews celebrated their Passover, this liberating event was meant to be recreated, to become vividly real again in the present, rather than merely recollected as a past event, the importance of which lay now in the past. Instead, the Passover meal was intended to bring home to the Jews the reality of their liberation, with all its implications for their lives as God's chosen people.

Similarly, in the Eucharist, the new Passover, Christ's liberating death can be said to be recreated, not in the sense of happening again as it happened on Calvary, but of happening again in a different way altogether. The couple who renew their marriage vows are not getting married as they did on their wedding day, but they are confirming and endorsing their marriage, and this confirmation and endorsement are qualitatively different from the couple saying to each other over an anniversary dinner how glad that they are they got married. By literally redoing what they did on that original day, they do in a very real sense return to that day which once again becomes a present reality. The wedding can't be repeated—and yet it can be. The look on the dead friend's face, caught so well by the camera, brings the friend vividly back to life, perhaps in a way even more vividly than when they were alive and the look was so familiar it was hardly noticed consciously. And yet, of course, the dead person doesn't come back to life nor is the look on the face there in the same way as it once was. Again, the evidence or the look on the witness's face, which the detective took no notice of at the time, may come back to him with such a force as to make it seem that he is hearing the words or seeing the look for the first time.

In the Eucharist, Christ's sacrificial death becomes a present reality, not in a literal physical sense since Christ cannot die again as He died on Good Friday, but in a quite different sacramental way. A historical event, like the crucifixion, happens only once, and yet like any significant historical event it remains in the historical consciousness as a present reality. What was achieved on the Cross for the world was achieved once and for all on that day and can't and doesn't need to be repeated. But what was achieved persists and remains as a victorious liberation which still affects the world. And so in the Eucharist this abiding, ever-present reality is commemorated in the sense of being re-presented by the repetition of the self-sacrificial words of Christ at the Last Supper when He anticipated His actual execution—"This is my body which is given for you" (Lk. 22:19) and "This cup which is poured out for you is the new covenant in my blood" (Lk. 22:20). Thus in the Eucharist as at the Last Supper, although now retrospectively rather than in anticipation, Christ offers up the Body and the Blood He shed for us on the Cross—yes, again and, of course, not again. The Eucharist can still be the same sacrifice of Himself that Jesus offered to the Father on behalf of the world without any blood being actually spilt, any actual physical flesh suffering. It is the same sacrifice like the Last Supper itself, but it is the manner of the offering which is different.

Can we find an analogy to help explain how this can be? Well, we can offer the same thing in different ways. I can offer my resignation by written words in a letter or by the spoken word. I can offer an apology to someone either through words, whether vocally or in writing, or by my actions or behavior. Thus a husband can apologize to his wife with flowers and without offering any words at all. I can offer a gift to someone either by giving him something or by giving him the money to buy it himself; or again, I might give him a check, a voucher, or a book gift certificate. But however I may choose to give the gift, the gift remains the same gift; it is just that the manner of offering it is different. To take another example, I may offer my congratulations to somebody either verbally or by presenting him with a medal or prize. To bring the analogy a bit closer, a man may offer his life for his country in a time of war in diametrically opposed ways. He may fight but, if he is a conscientious objector, he may volunteer for non-combative work which may be even more dangerous, like stretcher-work in a battle when he is defenseless and a sitting target. Or again, somebody may offer himself for extremely dangerous intelligence work behind enemy lines, with a far higher chance of being killed and tortured in the bargain. It is really not very difficult to find analogies to show that Jesus Christ can offer Himself in self-sacrifice in more than one way. And one doesn't have to believe that the Eucharist is a sacrifice because somehow, or rather in some utterly mysterious way, Jesus does get killed in the same way that He was killed on the Cross. Perhaps people, who cannot believe in the Eucharistic sacrifice, think that that is what the belief involves. Perhaps those who do hold the belief have sometimes given that impression by the explanations they have given of the doctrine.

Here we need to deal with an objection. An evangelical Christian may accept that the argument from analogy is persuasive, and yet still object that the argument doesn't touch the objection that the doctrine of the sacrifice of the Mass involves the idea that what happened at Calvary was not a unique event, a sacrifice offered once and for all time. Here again an analogy can help. To use the example of the present again, I can arrange with a wine merchant to send somebody a case of wine. But unlike when sending flowers, wine merchants are not in the business of enclosing cards with a message from the donor. Suppose that I wanted to be sure, as would be quite natural, that the element of surprise should not be spoiled by my sending a card revealing I was the giver until the wine actually arrived. But, not knowing the exact day of arrival, I send a card which arrives several days after the case of wine. In the meantime the person to whom I have sent the present remains in a state of suspense, not knowing who has sent them the wine, perhaps even wondering if there has been some mistake. So far as that person is concerned, the gift is not really fully received until my card arrives. There is an apparent present, but a present demands a giver and until the name of the giver is known, there is a very real sense in which my friend has received (it seems) a gift, but not my gift.

Well, analogies mustn't be pressed too far or too literally, especially when we are talking about God, but while Christ certainly saved me like all human beings, so far as they are willing to be saved, on that Good Friday when He offered His life for the world, nevertheless that liberating act still has to go on being *applied* not only to me but to all human beings. The human race continues to sin all the time. The medicine that the Cross provides has to continue being administered to the wounds of human nature. It is preeminently in the Eucharist that Christ re-presents, perpetuates, and applies the forgiveness and liberation which are the fruits of what He accomplished on the Cross once and for all. What was achieved, all that time ago, becomes especially in the Eucharist a present reality for the Church and the individual. Here another analogy may be helpful. A nation may celebrate each year some great battle or decisive war that gained or preserved their freedom from foreign conquest. The victory can't be repeated because the same battle or war can't be fought all over again, and yet every year the nation solemnly celebrates what is undoubtedly a historical event now in the past. Yet the event continues to reverberate, continues to be remembered with a more than academic gratitude, since, if the battle or the war had gone a different way, the nation would not now be free and independent. What happened in the past determines the present as an abiding reality. Every year that nation remembers, gives thanks, *and* celebrates their freedom with renewed appreciation. The victory is now history, but, nevertheless, it also dominates every day in the life of the nation. The prime example of such a victory celebration in this context is, of course, the Jewish Passover. But there is an important difference: the liberation of the Jews was not won by themselves but by God. Similarly, in the Eucharist the victory which is celebrated was not won by the people celebrating but by Christ.

The sacrifice which is offered up in the Eucharist, again, is obviously Christ's self-sacrifice and not the sacrifice of those offering and participating in the Eucharist. But there is also a significant way in which this sacrifice is, in addition and at the same time, the sacrifice of the human beings involved, who are after all members of Christ's own family. The Eucharistic sacrifice depends on the human agents who perform and take part in it. At this sacrifice, as in the Jewish "peace offerings," a communion between the divine and the human is effected when the participants eat "the Body" of Christ. But when they do this, something else happens. Let us use another analogy. We speak of a "body" of opinion, meaning there are a number of people who share a particular opinion. Similarly, we can also talk about the "body" of Christ, meaning all those who have Christ in common. Indeed, we can literally speak about them "sharing" Christ, since that is exactly what they do—very concretely—in the Eucharist. That is to say, they "live on," by eating and drinking, Christ's very self, His Body and Blood. They are not just the "body" of Christ because they share common beliefs about Him and share the kind of life He advocated—although they do that—but they do it as a necessary preliminary or condition for deeper and more personal sharing, the sharing of Christ Himself.

On the night before He died during the most extraordinary meal that has ever taken place, Jesus prayed to His Father that His followers would "all be one; even as thou, Father, art in me, and I in thee" (Jn. 17:21). We don't know what His apostles made of these mysterious words, but this wish was clearly not unconnected with the new Passover meal which He instituted on this last evening when He said goodbye to His apostles. For by consuming His Body and Blood, His adherents do indeed, in the most emphatic way, partake of the divine life. By "living on" this heavenly food which is Jesus Christ Himself, they necessarily enter into an extremely close relationship with the God of three Persons, as after all they cannot "live on" the Word, the Son of God, without also in some way entering the "family," if we may call it that, of the Trinity. Of course, it's not the only way that happens. As we have already seen, we are "adopted" as children of the Father when we receive the Spirit of Him and His Son. But it is certainly the most concrete way the relationship could be established in view of the fact that we are corporeal beings who have to eat and drink in order to live. It touches us because of the very physical and intimate act of eating and drinking.

We sometimes say that such-and-such is "food and drink" to someone, meaning it's just the kind of thing he loves, just the thing that keeps him going, so that we can say of someone, who has a passion for something, that it's his "life." In the same way, Christ is the "life" of His adherents, those literally who are "attached to" Him, and He is, not just metaphorically, their "food and drink." Because they not only hang on His words but actually live off His body in the Eucharist, they can be said to form the "Body of Christ" in more than a figurative sense. When, therefore, in the Eucharist they offer up the Body of Christ in sacrifice, they also inevitably at the same time are offering up themselves since they *are* the body of Christ. They offer their own lives in conjunction with His life which He sacrificed for them on the Cross. By uniting themselves in this way they associate themselves with His sacrificial self-offering, thereby sharing in His liberation of the human race.

We have talked about eating and drinking, but these basic human acts are often, or even normally, done with other human beings in the form of shared meals. Indeed, having a meal together has always been, in all societies, the most obvious and appropriate way for families, friends, and the community in general to meet together. Eating and drinking are essential for living, so to do it with our fellow human beings is the most natural thing in the world to do. Apart from doing this most basic and essential act in common, which provides such a convenient occasion for personal and social intercourse, there is something especially significant in sharing the same food and drink. In many cultures, in fact, this communal participation happens in a very literal way when all actually help themselves from the same dish or dishes and the same cup, as opposed to having their own separate portions and their own individual glasses. Such was the context in which the Last Supper took place when there was one cup and one loaf from which all ate and drank. When this is repeated in the Eucharist the same symbolism of union is preserved. For by sharing in the same loaf and the same cup, which become sacramentally the Body and Blood of Christ, a very clear unity is indicated and realized. The participants in the Eucharist are thus visibly united, not only with Christ, but also simultaneously with one another. So the Eucharist is "the sacrament of sacraments" not only because Christ Himself is present and received in the most real, that is, concrete of ways, but because by this feeding on the one Body and the one Blood of Christ that oneness of the human race, which was a key part of Christ's mission along with, and not separately from, restoring human union with God, is also "really" achieved in the most visible and least abstract of ways.

As well as being the most natural context for social intercourse on the ordinary daily level, meals are, in addition, the most obvious way of celebrating something. Significantly, the very first miracle worked by Jesus took place at a wedding feast. The extra wine that He procured by transforming water into wine was not only for the benefit of those guests. It was, like so many things both in the Old and New Testaments, a sign foreshadowing something far more important. In this case, of course, it was not the water but the wine at the Last Supper, which was to be qualitatively changed into something much more precious and wonderful than wine. The Last Supper and every Eucharist also anticipate an even more wonderful meal. And that is the ultimate meal, the eternal feast of heaven when human beings will be finally and irrevocably united in the closest of unions with one another and with God. It is that celebration of celebrations to which every Eucharist looks forward.

To conclude, the bread and wine that the ancient Jews offered in sacrifice to God in thanksgiving for the gift of food and drink took on a wholly new dimension in the Passover meal when, instead of the usual leavened bread, unleavened bread was eaten to indicate the haste with which their escape from slavery in Egypt was accomplished. The new Passover, in which Christ passes from this world to His Father, is celebrated and commemorated by Him in a meal in which the unleavened bread is now designated in such a way that it replaces the old lamb of the Jewish Passover—since the sacrificial lamb is now the very person presiding at the meal, Christ Himself. As for the special blessing of the wine which took place at the end of the Passover meal, that now becomes the blood of the new pact between God and His people—the Blood of Christ as opposed to the blood of a sacrificed animal which sealed the old pact between God and His chosen people. And finally Christ Himself clearly indicates that this transformed meal itself looks forward to an even more wonderful feast in heaven.

CHAPTER 17

THE WOUNDED CHURCH

Becoming a full member of the Church does not, unfortunately, guarantee that a person will be free of the temptations and weaknesses that belong to our humanity, which remains wounded by that inevitable orientation to sin that is our fallen condition. Not even the spiritual nourishment of "living on" Christ's Body and Blood can ensure complete immunity from the continuing effects of the diseased state in which we find ourselves.

Fortunately, however, there are two other healing sacraments which can be applied to the moral and spiritual wounds that we suffer as a result of our innate tendency to satisfy our own egos rather than attend to our real interests. The first of these is usually referred to as "Confession." It is also called "the sacrament of Penance" because of its penitential nature, or alternatively "the sacrament of Reconciliation" because its purpose is to reconcile.

To begin with, the obvious question that will be asked is: why is this sacrament necessary when a Christian can confess directly to the God of love who is all-forgiving? To go through another human being is surely not only unnecessary but actually undesirable, as it seems to deny the possibility of direct access to God as well as God's readiness to forgive without conditions or intermediaries.

The general answer to this objection is that it assumes a relationship with God which is not, in fact, the kind of relationship that Christ had in mind when He formed a new Chosen People. As we have seen, the uniqueness of the individual is not in question. What is in question is how the individuality of the person is best realized. Do I express myself most authentically and fully when I am isolated from my fellow human beings, or when I am in some sort of community and relationship with them? As we have already seen, in fact, the two things are not in opposition—whatever the tensions may be—because a situation of independent isolation is not one in which the individual flourishes. For we have a need of each other, both at the most basic level of day-to-day living and at the deeper level of a fulfilled life. For we were created not to live by ourselves but with one another. This life of community and relationship exists already in the God of three Persons who cannot be the God of Love unless there is Somebody to be loved.

When we were looking at how we are liberated by Christ's victory, we saw how we win our freedom, not all by ourselves, but as members of His Body. We have our own immediate, personal relationship with Christ, but this involves, rather than excludes, a close union with the other members of the Body. The belief in a God who is absolutely one and yet not monadic, but a community of Persons, is consistent with the understanding of human beings as at one and the same time unique individuals *and* members of a social community without which their individuality cannot flourish. Any view of society that sacrifices the individual person to some collectivist political philosophy—however well-meaning—is as inimical to Catholic Christianity as any privatization of the individual which denies social interdependency and the value of society to the individual.

When, then, we seek God's forgiveness, there is no reason why this should not involve others. There is a famous Russian novel in which a student for no reason whatsoever murders an old woman; having no religious faith he can't confess to a priest, but such is his guilt that he ends up by confessing to the chief of police. The overwhelming burden of having such a crime on one's conscience *demands* that one get it off one's chest to *someone*. In the case of murder there is no possibility of asking the wronged person for forgiveness; so one has to turn to someone else. Quite apart, anyway, from forgiveness, sin, especially serious sin, seems to call out for *sympathy* in the literal Greek sense of the word—*suffering with*. How can I murder somebody and not long to share my guilty secret with some other person if only somehow to ease the burden of suffering in isolation?

The fact is we need other people, and not least when we sin. It would not have been enough for that Russian student, even if he had been disposed to, simply to confess only to God. Confessing to God is inevitably an internal activity, but, necessary as it is, we as human beings with a social dimension need to externalize our innermost feelings and thoughts, and that requires communication with our fellow human beings. I was once on holiday, staying in a hotel, when I read in the papers about a terrible train crash. I was very afraid that it was the train a friend of mine took to work every day, but I didn't have with me his home or work telephone number. So, to ease the burden of my fears, I found myself almost involuntarily telling one of the hotel staff, a complete stranger. That's the way human beings are. We have a natural desire and need to share our joys, our fears, our sorrows—and our guilt.

There are two other reasons why a merely private confessing of our sins to God is not enough. If I say "sorry" to God, however sincerely and contritely, short of a miracle I am not going to hear any audible reply of forgiveness. There is, of course, an absolute need to say "sorry" to God and the spiritual relief of doing so is undeniable. And yet—as a social being I cannot help but want human input as well into my repentance. Is this just a weakness on the part of a fallen human being, lacking in faith? That's certainly one way of looking at it, and there would be some truth in it if admitting something to another human being were a way of letting oneself off the hook so far as God's concerned—if, in other words, it represented a kind of evasion, a means of not being confronted by the fact of having offended the God of Love. Well, anything can obviously be abused, but that no more removes the use than the saying, "the corruption of the best is the worst," implies that we should avoid the best. In fact, however, the humiliation of having to admit our faults to another person is more likely—although there may be exceptions—to increase our sorrow at what we have done, as well as to prove the sincerity of our contrition.

Anyway, if God created human beings not to live in isolation but to live in a close union both with one another and with Him, then there is nothing weak or indulgent in wanting to share my guilty secrets with another person, particularly if that person is empowered as a representative of the Church to give me God's forgiveness. For it is not just that there is an inevitable social dimension to life, but, as we have seen, God invites human cooperation, involves human beings in His plans, indeed depends in a sense on their help. The Church is His agency on earth, and her leaders, the successors of the apostles, together with their cooperators, are His agents and instruments. Jesus Christ cannot act on us through His Eucharist without their agency. In the same way, He uses them to convey His forgiveness to sinners. As we have remarked, Jesus didn't withdraw His mandate to cowardly, disloyal Peter when he disclaimed all association with Jesus, any more than He disowned the other apostles who didn't believe that He had risen from the dead even when eyewitnesses claimed to have seen Him. Awesome as the thought is, Christ gave enormous powers and responsibilities to His Church, and with the full knowledge—and indeed experience—that He would often be let down. Still, though, He continues to entrust the Church with His mission, just as God continues to allow human beings to look after His creation—often there, too, with disastrous results. If we ask why, then we are back to the problem of why God created us at all, and why He gave us free will.

The sacrament of Confession enables the members of Christ's Body to hear literally His words of forgiveness to the penitent sinner. He wants us to have this consolation just as He wants to give us Himself in the Eucharist so that we can "live on" Him. His methods are human, not inhuman. But apart from the comfort—and the Latin origin of the word reminds us that comfort is meant to be a strengthening not an enfeebling thing—there is another aspect to this sacrament.

The point about confessing to another human being is not only that it satisfies the human need for other people, and not only that it enables us to receive in a very concrete way God's forgiveness by actually hearing the words from His representative. There is the further dimension that sin is not only an offense against God but also against our fellow human beings. This is manifestly true of many or most sins, when we sin, more or less seriously, against our neighbor. But is it true of all sins? What about our most private acts and thoughts, which scarcely harm anyone else? This sounds like a plausible objection until we remember something I noted earlier in the book: namely, that the most personal of our actions which have no direct effect on anyone else, do unfortunately have an indirect effect. To think murderous thoughts is certainly not as bad, or the same as, actually murdering somebody. But we all know that the thought is father to the act. What we think today, we may do tomorrow. But even apart from that, whenever we do anything which is contrary to the human nature which is meant to be the image of the divine nature, we damage ourselves, we add to the wounds that prevent us from being the kind of persons God wants us to be, and consequently we do have a bad effect on other people. If we were isolated individuals, the latter would not be true. But because we are social human beings, interconnected and interdependent, nothing we do, however privately, is without its ultimate effect on others. The state of our hearts, the state of our minds, inevitably influences our external behavior, and that clearly affects other people. There is no isolating ourselves from others; no one is an island on his own.

And so in making our confession to another human being, we are confessing sins which are not only against God but also against our fellow human beings. Christ's agent, the Church's representative, consequently stands both for God and for any human beings we have offended, however indirectly and remotely. But not only do we need to make our peace with God and the human race, we also, as members of the Church, offend against the Church when we sin and, therefore, need to be reconciled with the Church, too. If I commit a murder, I have effectively broken off relations not only with God and the human family but also with Christ's Body, the Church. Such a serious sin necessarily excludes me from the community, into which I have to be reintegrated if I want to continue to be a Christian. It is not enough to say "sorry" privately to God, not enough even to make serious reparation to the dead person's family and to undertake heavy works of penance. I still need to make my peace with the Church to be admitted back into the family. For by my crime I have excluded myself; I am estranged from the community of love. I have become literally a stranger. To be reconciled to Christ requires being reconciled to His Body, the Church, and it is only by asking forgiveness that I can be welcomed back. One can't make one's peace with Christ without at the same time making one's peace with the People of God, where He is to be found and through which He is now present to the world. If the Church was nothing more than an association or fellowship to enable people who call themselves Christians to come together for worship, mutual aid, reflection, and so on—then no doubt the rupture which sin causes would not have all that much effect on our membership of a more or less voluntary association. After all, it is not something to which we are bound to belong by virtue of being a Christian. Such an idea of the Church assumes that there need not only be one Church; it is being a believer in Christ that counts not what Church one chooses to belong to. But, as we have seen, the Catholic understanding of the Church as the Body of Christ, united with Christ and united in herself as signifying that human unity which has been broken by sin, does not accept this separation of faith from Church—to be a Christian is to be a member of the new People of God. And therefore failings, especially serious failings, not only call into question one's identity as a Christian, but they also affect one's membership of the Church. To rupture one's relationship with Christ is at the same time to rupture one's relationship with His Church.

When we apologize to someone for something we have done, we naturally also want to make some amends if we are serious about being sorry. In small matters, the fact that we have taken the trouble to apologize, with the appropriate small gestures, may be sufficient amends. In larger matters we naturally want to express our sorrow by doing, as well as saying something. We want to substantiate our apology by putting ourselves out, doing something out of the ordinary. A neglectful husband may say it with flowers or by taking his wife out for dinner. A child may offer to help with the housework. In the case of a crime, a repentant criminal may wish to make some sort of reparation to the community. In sacramental Confession this reparation is called a "penance," which will vary according to the nature of the sin.

The subject of Confession arouses great, sometime almost envious, curiosity among non-Catholics. But I think it is true to say that the subject of "indulgences" provokes nothing more than incredulous contempt. And thanks to the fact that the abuse of indulgences was one of the key factors that triggered the Reformation, Catholics themselves, especially in non-Catholic countries, tend to be very embarrassed and even dismissive of them. But actually, like so many apparently strange doctrines and practices of Catholicism, they follow quite naturally from certain other facts, which are either not in dispute or which Catholics have no difficulty at all in defending when they are neglected or downplayed by fellow Christians. The insistence of Saint Paul, for example, that Christians are not isolated followers of Christ but interdependent members of His Body, the Church, means that just as in ordinary human society we depend on one another, so too, as Christians, we are not alone but helped by the other members of the Body. Now, as we have seen, some of these members who are dead but still very much part of the Church, in the heavenly as opposed to the earthly section, are people whose prayers are sought by those still on earth. Just as we naturally make use of the services of other members of the community in which we live without thinking that thereby we diminish ourselves, so too there is no reason why we should not make use of the achievements of the saints.

So what exactly is an indulgence? Well, first of all, it is not at all the same as forgiveness. We are forgiven by God in the sacrament of Confession, unreservedly. But as in human life the fact that somebody is forgiven is not quite the end of the matter, as we saw earlier. Our actions, both fortunately and unfortunately, carry consequences. If I do someone a good turn that is likely to have the effect, not only of that person being helped by my deed, but of making that person feel favorably disposed toward me, his gratitude is not the conclusion of the episode: a new or renewed relationship begins. On the other hand, if somebody does me a bad turn, my forgiveness is not quite the end of the affair. I may have no grudge at all, no desire for further apologies (if any have been given), no wish to punish the person concerned or in any way to have my revenge. Still, that doesn't mean that everything is as it was before. A relationship may have been damaged, a confidence shaken, and forgiveness does not alter that fact. Christians are expected to forgive, not to forget or turn a blind eye. We would be very foolish to go on trusting somebody who let us down badly. We don't want to go on making an issue of our disappointment, but what has happened has opened our eyes to an aspect of the other person's character which we hadn't realized before.

Well, in the same sort of way, God can forgive sin but what He can't do is to make its effects disappear—its effects, that is, on the sinner. The good things we do make us the kind of good people we are—but equally the bad in us makes us the bad people we are. Apart from anyone else, our sins affect us and help to make us the kind of people we are. By smoking one cigarette, we are drawn to smoke another one. Chain-smokers don't become chain-smokers overnight—the habit, the inclination, grows out of smoking individual cigarettes. A chain-smoker finds it extremely difficult to give up the habit because it isn't just a habit but an addiction. If I'm addicted to cigarettes, I can't stop smoking. If I'm addicted to chocolates, I can't stop eating them. If I'm addicted to drugs, then I am a drug addict. Some of us may feel that we don't have any addictions like that—but we would be wrong to think that. For the fact of the matter is that we are *all*, more or less, addicted to *sin*. We are drawn like a magnet to sins, whether big or small, because we have this strange suicidal urge in us which leads us to do things that don't make us happy and are not in our best interests. This addiction, which goes so contrary to that desire for happiness which is also innate in every human being, makes us the divided, utterly inconsistent, indeed ridiculous human beings that we are, so mysteriously busy working to make ourselves unhappy.

Just as the smoking of individual cigarettes forms a habit and can lead to an addiction, so the individual sins we commit lead to certain immoral habits, or worse addictions. If I steal once, then stealing the second time is easier than the first time; and the more I go on stealing the more the voice in my conscience becomes fainter, perhaps in the end inaudible. And the sin itself becomes a part of my personality, something that defines me (a thief), something without which I can't live. This fatal attachment to stealing may end in frequent spells in prison, which may persuade me, if not to feel guilty, at least to regret my addiction as something I would do well to overcome. All our egotistical attachments to self will ultimately, as we have seen, have to be ironed out of us before we will feel comfortable about going to heaven. Much, of course, can be done in this life. A real heartfelt conversion may remove any trace of attachment to the sin in question, in which case no purification after this life will be needed. But even if we don't manage to remove all attachment to a particular sin, still we can do much to reduce its hold on us by doing things to keep it at bay. The more good works we do to counterbalance its compelling attraction, the more we will do to dispel its fatal attraction, the more we will actually become a different kind of person for whom the temptation will cease to be a real "temptation" in the sense of being something that is attractive to us. We will be like the person who manages to give up smoking, and who can honestly say, in spite of the occasional desire for a cigarette, that he can't imagine now how he could ever have been so hooked on such a dirty and unhealthy habit.

We still, however, haven't explained what an indulgence is. We've only, so far, set the scene, the scene being the sediment that sin leaves in us. It is time to return to the great Catholic doctrine of the Body of Christ in which the different members, in the three different parts, are in contact with each other. Those in heaven obviously no longer need the help and support of those still on earth or those in the purificatory antechamber of purgatory, but they can certainly aid those in the other places. The spiritual "capital," so to speak, which has accumulated over the centuries in the Church, thanks to the holiness of the saints, amongst whom Mary is clearly preeminent, can't in one sense, of course, add *anything* to the spiritual "endowment" that Christ left to His Church, this endowment being the capital left to the Church after Christ's death on the Cross—which can never be exhausted, and which is ample by itself for all our needs. For if, as a famous poet has memorably put it, Adam is the "ruined millionaire" who lost the human race's endowment, then Christ, as the new Adam, has recouped, and, as we have said, more than recouped, what was lost in the "crash" when Adam and Eve squandered their fortune on a tip from the devil.

Nevertheless, as we have seen, human beings *are* invited to cooperate and to share in God's work of liberation—so that Saint Paul can even daringly say that he is helping to "complete" Christ's sufferings for the Church. Well, in one sense, of course, Paul can do no such thing—nobody can add anything to the complete victory won by Christ. But in another sense, it is meaningful for Paul to say that he is carrying on and sharing in Christ's work and, therefore, His sufferings. Consequently, the prayers and good works of all who have been faithful followers and so cooperators of Christ are part of the Church's accumulated capital on which all the members of the Church are free to draw. Not only is no Christian alone, but no Christian has, so to speak, his work cut out for him. Every Christian has to "earn his way," certainly, but equally every Christian has a common fund on which to draw. We might put it like this: an indulgence is granted by the Church when one of its members applies for a "grant" from this capital fund to pay off partly or wholly their losses incurred by their addictions to sin. In order to get this "grant" or indulgence, some penitential act of devotion or prayer or charity has to be performed; the value of this is then "topped up" by the Church out of its infinite resources. Gaining an indulgence doesn't take away the individual's responsibility, but it brings out the fact—the fact which the most Protestant of Christians are only too keen to stress—that the achievement is all Christ's and there is nothing we can do except receive from what He has won. All that the Catholic doctrine of indulgences adds to this is that we are invited to cooperate as coworkers of Christ and that, as Saint Paul himself says, we can add to what Christ has done in the sense—and only the sense—of continuing and sharing in Christ's mission. Saint Paul had never heard of an indulgence but, if it had been explained to him, he would have had no difficulty with what he was already in effect teaching—although the Church had not yet formulated the actual word or worked out explicitly the doctrine which is implicit in what Paul himself says.

Apart from Confession, there is another "healing" sacrament: literally, the Sacrament of the Sick. In this sacrament, Christ, once again through the agency of the Church, "touches" the sick person through anointing with oil, accompanied by prayer. The practice is attested to in the New Testament, and the Church, in view of Jesus' concern for the sick—a particular feature of Christianity and by no means so typical of other religions—has formally specified it as one of the official sacraments. Obviously, the sacrament is not given to somebody with a head cold. It is for those who are in danger of death through illness or simply old age, or for those already at the point of death. The strength, which the sacrament is intended to confer, is both physical and spiritual, aimed at the health of both body and soul.

There is always the possibility that real healing of the body will follow, but if not that, then the strength not to give in to discouragement and depression in the face of death. Indeed, the suffering can even be welcomed by the sick person. For, because of Christ's suffering on the Cross, because God by becoming man now knows through experience what our suffering is like (both mental and physical), human suffering is, as a result, changed and given a new significance. By willingly accepting suffering like Christ, human beings can actually share in the liberation and victory that Christ achieved and won through *His* suffering. Suffering ceases to be merely negative and acquires a positive value for the Christian. Naturally, to embrace, as opposed to resigning oneself to, suffering is not easy; the sacrament is meant to help the Christian to do this. If he is enabled to do this, he also helps to "complete" Christ's suffering on the Cross and thereby to share in His work. Thus the Christian life, which began with the anointings with oil of Baptism and Confirmation, ends with one last anointing to fortify the member of the Church in his move to a new part of the Church and a new life.

CHAPTER 18

THE LOVING CHURCH

So far we have looked at five sacraments, some at greater length than others, three of which are sacraments of initiation and two of healing. That leaves two other sacraments, which may be called sacraments of "service" because, although the people who receive them are meant to be strengthened by them, that is only because these particular sacraments are equally intended to be of benefit to others and to help build up the Body of Christ.

As I have already remarked, not all the sacraments can exactly be "proved" to be in the Bible. But those for which one can't actually point to specific texts, as one can most clearly for Baptism and the Lord's Supper, can be inferred from the New Testament. There is no sacrament for which one is forced to admit that there just isn't any justification for it in Scripture. But that said, one certainly couldn't *demonstrate* that marriage, to take perhaps the most obvious example, is "in the Bible" as a specific sacrament—but then one is also not going to find the word "sacrament" there, nor for that matter is one going to find the concept of sacrament explicitly explained. If the seven sacraments, which the Church of the first centuries came to recognize as authentic signs that make Christ's love effective, bringing it to bear both upon the individual Christian and the whole Body, aren't in fact what Jesus ever wanted—after all, if He had why didn't He say so plainly?—then it seems that the Spirit who was supposed to be leading the apostles into all truth either failed to do so or at any rate stopped doing so some time after the apostles' deaths. It would mean that, in spite of protests by a few forerunners of the Protestant Reformers, the Church had gone seriously astray in its teachings on the sacraments, thus deceiving its members until the sixteenth century when at last the voice of the true New Testament was once again raised by those Protestants who insisted that there were only two sacraments that were biblical—and that even they meant something very different from what the Church of both East and West understood by them. Both sides in this argument can adduce their respective biblical texts, but, at the end of the day, Catholics (and Orthodox) can admit that they can't *prove* their point from the Bible alone—but then there are a lot of other things which the Protestant reformers never denied, like the divinity of Christ, which can always be challenged by those intent on a different interpretation. So both sides are ultimately in the same position regarding the Bible. As we have said, a book doesn't speak for itself. The only difference is that those who reject the Protestant insistence on, as it were, cutting the sacraments down to size, wouldn't dream of resting on a written text alone, as the text "belongs to" the Church which alone decides what it means.

One of these two sacraments of service need not detain us long in a book about "mere" Catholicism. The sacrament of "Holy Orders," as it is called, is the sacrament whereby the mandate and mission entrusted by Christ to the apostles is perpetuated. We have already noticed how the apostles didn't hesitate, although apparently having no clear instructions from Christ Himself, to fill the vacant place left by the renegade Judas. Similarly, it was obvious that Jesus did not intend His Church to come to an end with the death of the apostles. It was, therefore, necessary to appoint successors to the original apostles. Furthermore, as the Church spread, it became evident that the twelve were no longer enough. Paul himself was not one of the first apostles. In due course, the successors to the apostles, called in Greek *episcopoi* or overseers, found that they needed helpers, and these collaborators were called, in Greek, "presbyters" or elders. These priests, as they came to be called, share in all the sacramental powers of the bishops apart from not being able to confer the actual sacrament of Holy Orders by themselves. Being auxiliaries of the bishops as opposed to being direct successors of the apostles, they don't have the same degree of responsibility for leading and Church and propagating her message. Finally, there is another class of auxiliaries to the bishops called "deacons," who have considerably fewer powers and responsibilities than the priests.

We must now turn, lastly but by no means leastly, to the sacrament of Marriage, a sacrament that calls for a great deal more comment. We have already noted a couple of significant points about Jesus' first miracle. We now need to emphasize the occasion rather than what happened on it. For it was at a *wedding* reception that this first miracle was worked. The context of what later could be seen as merely a kind of cryptic anticipation of something much more mysterious and wonderful, the turning of wine into blood as opposed to water into wine, was not at a birthday or a funeral or some special feast in honor of, or commemoration of, someone or something—but at a *marriage*. It doesn't require much imagination to realize that Jesus might be making a point—provided, naturally, one doesn't assume that Jesus went around doing things without any particular plan or purpose, but just haphazardly and without any special meaning. And furthermore, when we consider how the Old Testament begins with God enabling the marriage of Adam and Eve, while the New Testament ends with a vision of "the wedding-feast of the Lamb" in heaven, then marriage—which, as we have seen, Paul uses as the best image he can find for Christ's union with His Body the Church—begins to acquire a rather special significance.

When we reflect on what a sacrament means, we might well conclude, as we have done more than once in the course of this book, that we would have been tempted to call marriage a sacrament even without the Church telling us it is. For, after all, if a sacrament is a sign which effects that which it signifies, namely, some aspect of divine love, then marriage, that is, Christian marriage, has a very sacramental look about it. Created in the image of God who is Love, human beings are created above all to love. And there is no more intimate and personal a love than that between a man and a woman, which finds its physical expression in sexual intercourse. But, of course, it doesn't stop there because this lovemaking is potentially the source of new life. Thus human beings are enabled to be Godlike in another way apart from love: to be able to create new human beings. There is something else to notice about this lovemaking.

When a man and a woman copulate, they do, in a very obvious and physical way, become, literally, "one body." By being "joined together" in this way, they become the source of new life. That naturally doesn't mean that they cease to be two separate bodies—not at all. For the actual act, which at one and the same time constitutes both the most intense and satisfying physical expression of their mutual love for each other *and* the way in which they create babies, they do literally have to become physically "one." If they didn't do this, they wouldn't have a family, that is, a family of their own flesh and blood. If we remember what was said about God at the beginning of this book—the Trinitarian as opposed to monadic God—the analogy (as always only partial when we are trying to talk about the divine in human terms) is rather striking. The God who is Love has to have Somebody to love from all eternity and there is only one possible candidate: Himself. But far from this love being narcissistic—how could it be in the God who is Love personified?—it is not only directed at another Person, but this divine love "issues in" yet another Person who constitutes the mutual love of the other two Persons. The analogy obviously breaks down because the Spirit is not the child of the Father and His Word or self-expression, the Son, but is equally God with them. The child, on the other hand, although equally human with his parents, is not on an equal level insofar as the child is created and the parents are the creators. Still, there is a similarity with the mutual love of male and female which issues in children and which creates the family, a similarity which puts human marriage in a new light altogether.

We saw earlier how the three Persons who make up the one God are only different from each other in the different ways they relate to each other. For, although each is God, three in this (unique) case don't make three but one, there being only one God. The Christian understanding of the one God, whose life is nevertheless one of relationship, exactly fits—not unexpectedly since after all human beings are meant to be the image of God—what we know to be true of the human person who is both uniquely individual and also an essentially social being who can only exist in relationship with others. The most basic and fundamental of these relationships is that between a man and a woman. Without it, the race would cease to exist. Not surprisingly, the lapse of human beings into sin affected first of all this relationship. The first victim of sin according to the Old Testament was the marital relationship. After his fall from

God's favor, the original man immediately blames his wife for it. Recrimination is followed by the desire to dominate her.

Instead of conflict, men and women, different biologically, were intended to complement not undermine each other. Their physical differences are reflected in their different natures, potentially a source of support rather than tension. However, wounded human nature, damaged but not fatally, can still find in this relationship a powerful remedy for its ills. The close presence of another person helps, or can help, us to escape from the prison of the ego. Another person makes demands, and needs support. Another person of another gender, with more or less different strengths, adds a further dimension to the other spouse's life. True, some want to believe that little boys and girls, for example, only behave differently because of cultural conditioning. That was said to me once at an airport where I was with a family watching the planes landing and taking off. But as I watched their son pointing his toy gun at the aircraft while making distinctly belligerent noises and his small sister playing quietly and maternally with her doll, the explanation sounded unconvincing. The inescapable and determining difference between the two sexes is that only women can have babies but only through the action of men. Both sexes are totally dependent on each other for continuing the race. And their distinct reproductive roles dictate many other non-physical roles in which they complement each other.

Because human beings are constituted sexually as they are, but because they are also more or less crippled by sin, marriage is both utterly natural and at the same time hopelessly improbable. We need other people simply to live in the sense of exist. But we also need relationships, whether merely acquaintances or closer friendships, in order to live fully and happily. Sometimes we make lifelong friends but we all know that we form friendships that correspond to our particular stage in life and our circumstances. Not many of us keep up with our childhood friends throughout our lives. In many cases we probably can't even remember their names. Our friends at school are likely to be different from our friends at university, or the friends we make in our first job, and, if and when we get married, we may find ourselves, thanks to our husband or wife, consorting with very different kinds of friends from the ones we associated with before marrying. Now it's always sad, of course, to lose touch with old friends but most people cannot keep up with all the friends they have made during their lives. Some drop out of view, others we only manage to keep up with superficially through the annual Christmas card. And then, too, there are the friends we inevitably fall out with. That again is a sad fact about life, and we may often bitterly regret the falling-out.

But what is true of all these different friendships is that we never made any sort of promise or vow to be friends forever. If somebody I became friendly with asked me to swear lifelong friendship, come what may, I should be very taken aback. I might indeed be touched by the idea, even attracted by it, but still there would be something inherently odd and unrealistic about making such a mutual commitment. I might say, "Well, I do like you enormously and we certainly do get on terribly well together, but how can I possibly say how you or I will feel in a few years time? How do I know where I will be living, or where you will be living?" However, there is another, more serious reason why such an "engagement," so to speak, would be not only strange but even undesirable. Certainly, it would be perfectly in order for both parties to express the sincere hope and intention to be lasting friends. These things aren't often said, but they are implied in the relationship in all sorts of ways. So, why would it be inappropriate to ask for or to give such a binding commitment?

Well, we might not yet be married, but if we do get married we would have to take account of our husband's or wife's likes and dislikes; in the interests of marital harmony we might have to see our friend much less than before. Or again, we might move to a new job, and our friendship might have rested very much on the fact that we had much in common through our work. Or we might move away, and telephone conversations aren't quite the same as meeting in the flesh. Of course, there are friendships that last through thick and thin, never cease to be close and intimate, but they are the exception rather than the rule in the sense that lifelong friends either congratulate themselves on the way they have kept up with each other or alternatively thank the circumstances that enabled them to stay close to each other.

Now this might prompt us to reflect that that's increasingly the situation in a secularized society where divorce is becoming the norm rather than the exception. Is marriage really any different from friendship? Is it not simply a sexual friendship, so to speak, which either partner is free to end when it suits him or her? One doesn't expect people to go through their lives with the same friends, never to lose friends, or never to make new friends. Why should it be any different with marriage? A man, who meets a woman, is attracted by her, falls in love with her, and enjoys her company, may have had quite a limited experience. Even somebody who has known many women hasn't known them all. There are still millions of women out there he has never even met. How can he possibly know that he won't meet somebody who is more attractive, more loveable, potentially a better mother than his present wife? And the same, of course, is true for his wife. It is equally true that the longer they are married and living together, the more they discover about each other. And not only that, for although they are married, they still remain their own separate selves, developing, growing older, and maturing in their own ways. After some years they may feel that they are really quite different people from the people they were when they got married. Doesn't all this go to show how utterly unrealistic, indeed impossible, it is to believe that marriage can be a lifelong commitment. Friendship isn't; why should marriage be any different?

The Jews in Jesus' time allowed a man to divorce his wife. Some religions permit polygamy, which has the advantage of providing security for spouses who may find themselves out of favor. But all cultures and societies have at least implicitly acknowledged that it is undesirable for people just to have more or less transient sexual relationships. And here, of course, one major difference from friendship is that copulation can lead to children who cannot fend for themselves. Even in the most fiercely secular society, where promiscuity has practically established itself as a recognized way of life, there is also a recognition that children need security and a parental care which is stable. Also there is the uncomfortable feeling that having children does ideally, at least, require some sort of permanent arrangement, whether one calls it marriage or not. Even among the most promiscuous people, there is some desire to settle down with one partner. Even where contraception has also become the norm, there is, especially and naturally among women, some desire to have children. People, whatever their own unstable background (or perhaps particularly because of), whatever their own infidelity, are likely to entertain some dream, some hope, that their marriage will last.

The fact of the matter is that sexual friendship is not the same as ordinary friendship. That is not at all to say that the element of friendliness is necessarily greater, but it is to say that the physical closeness and intimacy with its capacity to generate new life makes it altogether different. It implies marriage, and everyone knows that in their hearts, whether they want to use the word or not. It is true that, when a man and a woman lie together and become one physically, they aren't by any means necessarily one in other ways. Saint Paul says that when they are joined bodily the "two shall become one," but Paul was recommending a course of action not describing an automatic state of affairs. And yet he certainly wasn't saying something odd or revolutionary, something that he could have only thought of because of Jesus Christ. Human beings need and depend on each other; there is a natural desire to draw closer to others rather than to retreat into one's own shell. And when two people lie together, there is an implicit assumption that if they are not together, "one," in other ways too, then they are lying with their bodies. The most extreme example of such lying, so blatant that lying ceases to be the appropriate word, is prostitution, where the assumption is precisely the opposite— that neither party has any interest at all, in fact quite the reverse, in togetherness and oneness in anything but the physical sense; indeed one party hasn't even any interest in that. Prostitution has always existed in all societies, but equally its depersonalizing inhumanity has always been recognized. There is no behavior that is more inauthentic.

But even if the coming together in physical union of two bodies cries out for an equal coming together of two hearts and minds, that still doesn't solve the problem with which we began: how can we expect two people to stay together as one for the rest of their lives when we certainly don't demand it of even the closest of friends? The difficulty of it has been universally accepted, which is why the religions of the world, and why society itself, has laid down laws and norms to stabilize marriage. These vary in strictness and morality, with women usually coming off worst. Clearly, the less strict the restrictions, the easier, the less improbable, marriage appears to be.

The more the oneness is qualified, the less demanding marriage becomes. The fact that Christ made the highest demands—criticizing the comparatively lax Jewish practice which He called a concession to the hardness of the human heart—may be seen as robbing Christian marriage of all practical chance of success. Why should any man get married when he's stuck with only one wife and with no chance of getting rid of her? Isn't this to demand too much of human frailty?

The objection suggests the answer, which is that Christ came into this world to raise us out of our frailty, to give us a new lease of life, to give us the spiritual heart transplants that fallen human beings so desperately need if they are to have any chance of leading the sort of life they were intended to live. Marriage is only one particular example, albeit a very important one, of the human dilemma—that dilemma which consists of the contradiction between our sense of what is right and ideal, on the one hand, and, on the other hand, our helplessness in living up to what, in our fallen state, we still know to be right in our hearts and consciences. Not hopelessly bad, except through our own fault, we still have this fatal orientation toward doing what we are aware, more or less clearly, we should not do. So how does the ideal of lifelong, monogamous marriage become a more realizable possibility by being understood as a sacrament?

Naturally, there are marriages which endure happily without any specific Christian understanding. There are couples so admirably suited to each other that the marriage seems, as they say, to have been made in heaven. In these cases, there is little temptation to selfishness because both parties want, more or less, the same thing. But in the majority of marriages there is, to a greater or less extent, a conflict between two egos, with potentially fatal results. The reconciling element that the sacrament offers introduces a new dimension. In the chapter after next we will look at how, if at all, Christian morality differs from any other morality, but we can anticipate that discussion here by pointing out that, where a belief in Christ's self-sacrifice on the Cross is at the center of a person's life, that life does have a different dynamic from a life in which this is absent. If the liberation of the human race was won by the ultimate sacrifice of sacrifices, the loss of a person's life, then self-sacrifice takes on a very special meaning and significance in the scheme of things. Instead of being against a person's interests, as the fallen human mind automatically supposes, self-sacrifice comes to be seen as a disinterestedness which is very much in a person's real interests. Paradoxically, what is selfless turns out to be a matter of self-interest.

In marriage freely undertaken, a man and a woman offer their bodies to each other in the most intimate of ways. But if the self-giving stops there, then the marriage only exists on that physical level. This assumes, of course, that sexual intercourse is intended to be an expression of affection and love, as the physical actions suggest. It is certainly the most concrete manifestation of marriage that there is—without it there may be companionship and friendship but there is no marriage. That suggests that the physical self-giving is the key to the thing. And one doesn't have to be a Christian to think that. It is perfectly possible for the human mind to work that out without any help from any religion.

But that doesn't remove the difficulty of achieving what is seen as desirable. The self-giving that is crucial to the health of the relationship is not easy for morally disoriented human beings. And this is where the Cross of Christ comes in, as in the sacrament of Marriage it casts its shadow, or rather its light, over the relationship. Imitation is, it is said, the highest form of flattery, and the Christian will, therefore, be interested in following the example of Christ, given that His example is believed to be the act that completely and decisively changed the history of the human race. Without this element of self-sacrifice, one is tempted to say that no marriages, except those in which cultural, religious, or social pressures effectively prevent separation and divorce, can, humanly speaking, survive, except on a purely external level. And indeed this is the testimony of modern secular Western society, where hardly any inhibitions now exist, apart from financial ones and concern for the children of the marriage. Even in this milieu there is still general regret when marriages fail, not least because of the practical consequences for those involved. Nobody actually thinks divorce is a positive good—just an unfortunate necessity.

What the *sacrament* of Marriage does is to transform a situation where the desirability of marriage is recognized but where the associated difficulties are also seen as more or less overwhelming. The centrality of self-sacrifice, as the key to human happiness and liberation, has another aspect. For while Christ gave up His life for the whole human race, more particularly He gave it up for His Body, the Church. The marital significance is clear, since a loving, as opposed to an exploitive, sexual relationship means giving one's body to another person, as opposed to forcing it on or submitting it to somebody else's body. And so marriage as a sacrament only reflects the loving relation between Christ and His Body. It also reflects the *oneness* of Christ and the Church, which is *His* Body. The husband and wife are also intended to become one both on the physical and the spiritual levels. By literally uniting their bodies they become one body, with the result that each's body becomes the other's body too, and the care one has for his or her own body is extended to the body of the other. A care and concern is to be reflected in all the other aspects of their lives together. Just as Christ makes the Church holy, so marital union is meant to raise the spouses to a higher life of self-giving, always in imitation of Christ's self-giving. As a sacrament, it not only reflects or signifies but it also makes effective this self-giving in the lives of the two people. Their fidelity to each other—against all the human odds—reflects, in addition, the faithfulness of God to His people whom He never deserts, again against all the odds, so to speak, given the faithlessness of human beings.

Given that marriage is a sacrament, we may ask who "performs" it, since sacraments don't just happen. Not all sacraments require a priest; Baptism doesn't, for example. But even so, we can't baptize ourselves; somebody else has to. However, in the case of marriage the only people who can "marry," that is, make the sacrament work, are the two people getting married. True, Church law demands that one of its agents, a priest or a deacon, has to be present to give it the Church's formal blessing and recognition. But that official endorsement by the Church is not enough, whereas in the case of the Eucharist, for example, the sacrament takes place regardless of the people who are there, provided it is celebrated properly by a successor of the apostles or one of his collaborators (priests). A wedding may take place in church with all pomp and ceremony, but that doesn't necessarily mean that a *marriage* has also taken place, for a wedding is not exactly the same as a marriage.

For instance, the bride may be pregnant and only going through the ceremony out of fear of her parents. She says the right words, but she doesn't mean them at all. In fact, she doesn't actually want to marry the bridegroom. Indeed, she does not intend to marry him. She is really not getting married but going through an empty ceremony to please her parents. Whatever the intentions of her bridegroom, she herself is saying words that she doesn't mean. Her words state that she gives herself to her husband as his wife and takes him as her husband. Yet if she doesn't mean what she says, she is not marrying him.

Take another example. A bridegroom may say the critical words in church, but what he means by them is that he would like a sexual relationship with his wife, maybe leading to children, but that he reserves the right to put an end to the marriage if, as may well happen, his love for her cools over time, or somebody more attractive comes along. Again, he is not meaning what the Church understands by the words or vows, since they imply a lifelong commitment. That is what is meant by the idea of a "husband" who is by no means the same as simply a sexual partner. Or again, the bridegroom may very much want children and believes that it is essential for their happiness that the marriage is lasting, but, on the other hand, he may not think that precludes having another wife on the side. In that case, he too doesn't mean what the Church means by marriage, a relationship which is by definition monogamous. Yet another bridegroom may be absolutely sound on commitment and monogamy, but have such a horror of children that he has no intention of allowing his wife to have them. This wedding also wouldn't qualify as a marriage because the Church understands children to be the natural outcome of a marriage. The idea of marriage is that it leads creatively and outward to family, rather than inward. Perhaps, on the other hand, both bride and bridegroom intend all the elements we've mentioned so far, but unfortunately one of them has a horror of sex or is inhibited for some reason from consummating the marriage. Sadly, in that case also, a perfectly regular wedding would not be the public expression of a truly marital relationship, since for husband and wife to be one it is necessary that they be one physically.

Without exhausting all the negative elements that stop a wedding from being a marriage, enough has been said to show that this sacrament is rather more complicated than the other sacraments. It is true that in certain sacraments such as Eucharist and Holy Orders there is some dispute as to exactly at what point the sacrament "takes," but still one can isolate a particular action accompanied by words, more or less. But in the case of marriage, although one can certainly point very precisely to a particular moment in the wedding when the man and woman commit themselves to each other as husband and wife, the words by themselves are not enough. For it is not enough even for the two people to mean what the Church means by the words. A certain physical action has to take place outside the public wedding in a very private setting.

Finally, listing some of the factors involved in this sacrament enables us to understand what the Catholic Church means by annulments. These have a very bad press, it has to be said. And it has to be conceded that the process of annulment, like all legal processes, is a human business involving fallen human beings, without there being any question of the Church's infallibility being involved. Witnesses may lie in Church courts, and judges are fallible human beings. Whether a marriage never really took place is known only to God. There is a well-known English expression that "the law is an ass," and everybody can subscribe to the sentiment but without thereby implying that the law should be abolished. Like all things human, it is flawed because human beings are flawed. But that is not a reason for abolishing it any more than any other human institution. We should be in a sorry state without it, as anyone who has lived in an anarchic society can testify. Church law is no different, although one would expect it to be less flawed than a system not inspired by the same ideals. Insofar as the process is cumbersome or incompetent, the Church has fallen down. But no amount of human error, or worse, can remove the fact that not all weddings represent real marriages, so the alternative to annulment is either forcing two people to remain in an inauthentic relationship, or else just permitting them to divorce as though a true marriage were being ended. For divorce implies an existing marriage, whereas annulment implies no marriage. There is a world of difference, and the possibility of annulment is essential both to safeguard the integrity of the sacrament and to protect innocent people.

CHAPTER 19

DOES MY BODY BELONG TO ME?

The answer to the question, "Does my body belong to me?" seems obvious enough. To whom else, after all, *could* it belong? And yet the question isn't as silly as it sounds. For my body does not belong to me in the way that my umbrella does. It is not something external to me which I possess like an umbrella. It makes perfectly good sense to point out to somebody that that umbrella belongs to me; whereas to announce that this eye belongs to me sounds very strange indeed. And, of course, the reason is that my eye is a part of me, unlike my umbrella. One could, it is true, have an artificial limb, for example a leg, which could be detached from one's body and to which one could point and say, " This artificial leg belongs to me." But my body and its natural constituent parts are not like that. They are not appendages of me; instead they help make up the person I am, since I am a corporeal as well as a spiritual person.

It is paradoxical that the less religious or the less spiritual people are, the more inclined they are to treat the body more like an umbrella. They tend to regard the body as something which belongs to them in the sense that it is there for their pleasure and use. The body ceases to be something important, to be taken seriously in its own right, and becomes more like a possession at one's beck and call. It is available for whatever purpose one chooses to put it. The only restriction is that one can't use it to harm others against their will. But for those who see the human body as part of God's creation, the body, in a very real sense, still belongs to God and is not a disposable asset. Moreover, because the body is created by God, rather than being just a collection of molecules that have emerged somehow or other from complex chemical interactions, it is presumably designed with particular functions and purposes in mind.

When we come to God's plan for the body, we encounter what have probably become the strongest objections to Catholicism, at least in Western secular society, where the body increasingly is regarded as something that is there for our convenience and satisfaction. With the exception of using it for recognizably anti-social purposes, society upholds that it is entirely our business as to what use or non-use we make of the body. This is, obviously, especially true of sexuality. That Catholicism would come to be seen as the great foe of the emancipation of the body would certainly have greatly surprised our ancestors, including the Protestant Reformers. What is now regarded as a peculiarly Catholic intolerance in matters of the body was, until quite recently, the general attitude of society. Certainly, this is still the Catholic position that what the Church teaches on sexual morality is in no way dependent on Catholic belief but is simply part of the Natural Law, which you don't need to be a Christian, let alone a Catholic, to accept. The Natural Law is the moral law, which unaided human reason can grasp without any sort of revelation. These basic moral truths may not be immediately clear to the reason, but that is because reason doesn't function as well as it should, due to the fact that human beings are morally flawed. This is where religion comes in, to enlighten and strengthen our reasoning powers.

When we look at the body, it is clear that its sexual organs are designed for intercourse with a member of the opposite sex. It is equally obvious that the sexual interaction of male and female is necessary for human beings to be born. But unfortunately—and people do recognize that it is unfortunate if only because this is the only way men and women can have children—there are many people, even though a small minority of the human race, who are not naturally attracted to the opposite sex. In some cases, this may be the result of deliberate choice on their part. But it is not known whether people have homosexual or lesbian orientations because of genetic factors, family background, or both. For these people, it is argued, heterosexual sex is not natural. So, the argument continues, they should be entitled to use their genitals in the way that appeals to them. Of course, neither the Bible nor the Christian tradition supports this argument. Nevertheless, there are Christians who argue that the biological facts justify a change of attitude and that, therefore, they are justified in manifesting their love in the way appropriate to them. How can one demand of them what amounts to celibacy if they have no call to it?

The appeal of this approach is extremely powerful, and to resist it can easily appear both intolerant and judgmental. And before saying anything further, it is important to remember that judging an action to be wrong is not at all the same as judging the person. The only person I am entitled to judge is myself, since I am the only person about whom I have sufficient knowledge. I cannot get into another person's conscience; I don't know all their circumstances or the pressures they are under. I simply cannot judge the guilt of another person. Furthermore, if I do condemn somebody else, I am quite likely committing a worse sin than he or she, so I would be better employed judging myself.

There is, however, a problem for a Christian who would embrace the "enlightened" view of homosexuality lifestyle. Where does he stop? For example, what about a husband whose wife becomes frigid or disinclined to sex? He too is condemned, perhaps at a comparatively early age, to a life of celibacy. How can that be fair to him? And yet he solemnly married his wife "for better or worse," so, when the "worse" comes along, he has committed himself to enduring it. Or again, what about a man who is extremely attractive to and easily attracted by women? Is it fair to apply the law of monogamy to him? After all, he is tempted and given "opportunities" more than other men. Oughtn't there to be a different standard for him? And then what about the kind of person who finds any sort of commitment, let alone permanent commitment, extremely difficult? For him transient sexual relationships may be quite "normal." Even more serious: what is to be said about those who are so mentally or physically handicapped as to be unable to marry? How could God create human beings who cannot make use of their sexual organs as they were intended to do?

In fact, it is absurd to view homosexuals as a special class all by themselves, for whom an exception can be made to the traditional

Christian teaching that our sexuality is intended for monogamous marriage between a man and a woman. If there is a problem, it is not a problem about homosexuality but a problem about creation: how God could create a world in which evil and pain could arise.

Again a woman's body, to turn to another area in which Catholics are attacked for intolerance, is not hers to do with exactly as she pleases. If, as a result of sexual intercourse, she conceives, she has to face the consequence of her action. The life that is conceived in her is not hers to dispose of as she pleases. In that sense, her body does not "belong" to her. It is not like a material instrument which she can use as she pleases.

It is difficult to imagine anyone actually being positively in favor of abortion, which can never be seen as anything other than a necessary evil. Some people, who are generally opposed to abortion, want to make an exception for rape, where clearly conception is not the result of a voluntary action. To have been raped, they argue, is bad enough, without having to give birth to an unwanted child. While it is true that the woman is not obliged to bring up the child but can arrange for an adoption, this does not remove the suffering she has to undergo in giving birth. There are many who are opposed to abortion but will say that here we have an exception to the general rule. But rape does not change the fact that a living person has been conceived.

There is an unborn child here who is like any other fetus and is not responsible for how it came to be. As with homosexuality, if we try to make an exception here, we are faced with other possible exceptions, all of which can be justified on similar, if less pressing, grounds. Once you believe that unborn life cannot be destroyed, there cannot be any exceptions. Christians who defend exceptions are guilty of inconsistency. After all, if they are Christians, they believe in the Cross of Christ and the liberating effects of voluntarily accepting suffering. From the Christian point of view, a woman in a situation like this is faced not with physical death but with another kind of living death. And if she is a Christian, she is asked to accept this cross, and if she does so, not only will she literally bring new life into the world, but also her sacrifice will be the source of new life to her, and, through her example, to others. This obviously assumes that Christianity's unique belief in the value of suffering is true. As so often in the course of this book, it appears that Catholicism is only the logical extension of basic or "mere" Christianity.

However, the fact that a person's body doesn't belong to him or her to dispose of as desired doesn't mean that a person hasn't the right to defend his or her body against attack. In a time of war, for instance, there is no reason, in principle, from the Catholic point of view why a woman threatened with rape should not use artificial contraceptives to prevent conception, provided they are not also abortifacient. This may surprise people, but the Church's view of contraception relates to marriage where two people freely give themselves physically to each other in a potentially creative act. Nor is the Church against birth control, as is often supposed. It approves of natural as opposed to artificial methods. There are many people who would agree with this on health rather than moral grounds. Would anyone, after all, want to swallow pills, which like all drugs, have possible side and long-term effects—when they could be using natural means? It is hard to imagine anyone so wanting. The Catholic position is not so peculiar as many suppose.

There are indeed people who have a contraceptive approach to marriage, never intending to have children. One doesn't have to be a Catholic to see that as an unnatural attitude. As we have seen, the Church can't budge on this principle if only because a willingness to have children is one of the conditions for a marriage being a sacrament. Nor is it only a question of artificial contraception. The same is true of using natural methods: a couple who only believe in alternative medicine, for example, might reject contraceptives on totally non-ethical grounds. But if they also refused to have children, they too would be depriving their marriage of a sacramental meaning, even though they never touched artificial contraceptives. Or again, they might limit their family for purely materialistic and selfish reasons without obviously going against Catholic teaching on contraception.

If our bodies are not ours to do with as we choose, that also includes depriving our bodies of life. Here again, as with contraception, we can't limit our moral judgment merely to a physical act divorced from its context. Not every killing is murder. Some killings are wrong but not as serious as murder, such as manslaughter. Others are entirely blameless as in accidents when the perpetrator is wholly innocent. By no means is everybody who takes their lives by suicide guilty of serious sin. Far from it. Possibly the majority of people who put an end to their lives do so when their minds are unbalanced. And there are other cases, where the person may not be mentally ill or disturbed but where he acts under extreme pressure, such as fear of suffering from some terminal illness. A Christian who has faith and hope, with the model of Christ's passion before him, will be in a very different position from an unbeliever. More is expected of the believer. But all these cases are totally different from the true suicide, when somebody takes his own life deliberately, fully aware of the damage it will do to others—indeed, perhaps doing so for the very purpose of hurting those closest to him.

Similarly, the Catholic opposition to euthanasia should not be interpreted as meaning that anyone who lets somebody die is necessarily doing something immoral. A decision to discontinue a medical treatment that is out of proportion to any real result it can achieve is perfectly acceptable, just as there is nothing wrong in giving painkillers to a dying person even if it has the effect of shortening his life—in fact, it would be cruel not to do so. What euthanasia, in the objectionable sense, refers to is deliberately shortening a life which was created by and belongs to God, for whatever apparently good reason. We are not required to artificially force a dying person to go on living. But equally, it is not justified for anyone to decide that a certain amount of suffering justifies ending a life. After all, suffering is relative. I may not think that handicapped person has much of a life, but I cannot put myself in the position of a handicapped person. My own life may not appear to be much of a life to somebody else, but I may not take that view. Obviously, asking someone to put an end to my sufferings is very different from deciding that somebody else's sufferings are such as to justify the ending of his life. But the principle is the same—and the step from one to the other is not so big. Again, the same considerations apply as in the case of suicide. I cannot judge someone who, in intense pain, asks that his life be terminated. It may well be that his mind is disturbed. Different cases of euthanasia will vary considerably in their degree of seriousness, just as murders are by no means all equal in gravity. A cold-blooded murder to take possession of one's wife's money can hardly be compared with the desperate act of a jealous lover acting in a fit of passion.

Catholic teaching on all these matters I have discussed here has become increasingly unfashionable and unpopular in Western secular society. But this teaching does not claim to be based on revelation, it claims to be based on reason, reason that can discover the moral law unaided by any Christian or any religious belief. Our human reason can work out what the body is designed to do, that it has been given genitals for intercourse between man and woman, an intercourse which naturally leads to new life; just as it can tell us that the human destroying of human life must be an inhuman act, whether it is killing an unborn child or an elderly or very sick person. But reasoning is not an automatic process. Somebody has to do the reasoning and that is a human person, a person endowed with conscience but also a sinful person. A person may reason more or less conscientiously, with a greater or lesser degree of responsibility, more or less under the influence of self-interest or what is perceived to be politically correct. Reason, therefore, can go disastrously wrong, especially where it is unaided by religious belief and a sense of being answerable to a Creator. But ultimately, the modern secular world's hostility to Catholicism is not a hostility to its revealed doctrines but a hostility to reason itself.

CHAPTER 20

ARE CATHOLICS
BETTER THAN OTHER PEOPLE?

If there is any truth in the argument of this book that "mere Christianity" adds up to Catholicism, the question that then suggests itself is whether this means that Catholics are the real Christians whose lives are bound to be better than those of other people. However, the slightest observation will show that Catholics are not at all necessarily better than others. All that could be said, because of their beliefs, is that they *should* be better than their neighbor. Clearly, however, their practice all too often falls below their profession. We need, though, to be clear in what way Catholics who live up to their ideals can be expected to behave better than others.

As has already been pointed out, it is certainly not part of Catholic teaching that Christians are in the possession of a moral code which is not available to their fellow human beings. On the contrary, conscience and reason are universal, and it is possible, at least in theory, for anyone to know what the so-called Natural Law dictates. For that is what the term implies: that knowledge of it is natural to human nature. But because of human frailty and sin, it is also true that conscience and reason can be blinded or blunted. Here any religion which faithfully reflects the Natural Law can be a salutary teacher. If Christ, then, didn't reveal a morality hitherto unknown and unknowable, what did He add to the picture?

After all, the concept of charity or love was not absent from the morality of Judaism. No, the dimension Christ added was an altogether new dynamic enabling human nature to live according to the moral law in a way it had never before been able. What was lacking previously was not the letter but the Spirit. And this lack put the Jews, whose religion ensured that they had a moral awareness which was lacking to their neighbors, into the unfortunate position of knowing what they ought to do, while at the same time being more or less powerless to do it because of the fatal orientation of handicapped human nature. What Christ makes available is a Spirit which can move the heart and make human beings capable of doing what they had not the motivation of doing before. It was this Spirit, this Holy Spirit, which the most insightful of the Jewish religious teachers had realized God must provide if He expected frail human beings to behave according to their original nature as He had created it.

But that was not all that Jesus did. Although it is true His own moral teachings do not exactly add anything that could not have been known before, that doesn't mean that He didn't add anything. He did. He drew out the implications of the Ten Commandments in His Sermon on the Mount. He released, as it were, their hidden potential, making clear what follows from them, what demands they make on the human heart, since external actions proceed from the interior dispositions we have. By internalizing the moral precepts of the Ten Commandments, Jesus reveals their full meaning. So in a way nothing is added, and yet something very important is added. And what is added can only be properly realized through a new orientation of the human heart, which is where the Spirit comes in. For while no new commandments are given, a deeper and more profound response to them is called for by means of an internal revolution. This revolution involves a radical change of heart, the source of all human actions and behavior. Above all, the Spirit transforms hearts into loving hearts.

The world, in fact, implicitly acknowledges this moral revolution. It recognizes the distinction between a "good" and a "Christian" action or work. There is a difference between simply feeding a starving person and feeding him kindly and lovingly. Everybody knows what a Christian act is, but what would a Buddhist or a Hindu or a Jewish or a Muslim act be? Presumably it would be a moral or virtuous act, but such an act need not be a loving act. It is possible to do a great deal of good, even heroic good, but in a merely dutiful or even condescending way. There is no doubt about the value of the acts, even when done without love, but the recipients will not love the doer in return. Indeed, those who benefit from other people's aid are often left resentful rather than grateful. And it is quite true that the very word "charity" may leave a nasty taste in people's mouths, but that is because the help that is on offer appears more patronizing than compassionate. "Charity" in that case will be a parody of the real charity which is associated with Christianity. Of course, you don't have to be a believing Christian to behave in a Christian way. The Spirit is not confined in that way. But even when you hear it said of somebody of another religion that he is very Christian in his behavior, or even more Christian than the Christians, that still reflects a recognition of the moral revolution that Jesus brought about when He proclaimed that the whole of morality was summed up in the one word "love."

It is often said that you don't have to be religious to be good, but that depends on what you mean by "good." If you mean simply virtuous, then that is perfectly true. Far from denying it, Catholicism has always maintained that the moral law is knowable by anybody if they use their conscience and reason properly. You don't need the Christian revelation or the Catholic Church to discover the moral law. But that doesn't alter the fact that the Christian revolution has affected the meaning of the word "good." Christians may only be a minority of the world's population, but the message has nevertheless "got through." The world may be largely ignorant of Christian beliefs, but the one thing it does know is that a Christian is supposed to be a loving person. That is precisely why the world comes down so hard on Christians when they are perceived as acting in an unchristian way. Other religions may, for instance, approve of executing adulterers, but, although Christianity also condemns adultery, it would be considered very unchristian if a so-called Christian country resorted to such a drastic penalty. After all, one aspect of this Christian love is known to be forgiveness, which is a quality not associated with other religions or humanist philosophies of life. So, certainly, it's perfectly possible to be "good" in the sense of virtuous or dutiful, but that's not the same as being compassionate, forgiving, and loving.

It is also significant that the Catholic Church in particular attracts a great deal of bad publicity when it is perceived as having failed to live up to its ideals and principles, for the world is very well aware of what these ideals and principles are. No other body has been criticized so strongly—and so unfairly—for its alleged failure to protest against Hitler's holocaust of the Jews. The secular world expects popes to act heroically in defense of humanity. It knows that Catholic Christianity proclaims the ideal of self-sacrifice. It doesn't expect secular humanists to risk their lives in defense of the weak and helpless, but it does rightly expect Christians, and above all Catholics, to do so. The fact that it does is revealing. For it shows that it is appreciatively aware of the self-sacrificing heroism which Catholic Christianity exemplifies at its best. It may profess critical skepticism about men and women who embrace a way of life which entails celibacy, obedience, and poverty but, interestingly, it assumes that such eccentric people will be prepared to risk everything when the circumstances demand it.

The world also is well aware that what underlies this willingness is something that is called "faith." And the paradox is that, while the behavior which depends on this thing is considered admirable, the thing itself, faith, is dismissed as incredible, that is, literally unbelievable. Yet the kind of person who says that he couldn't possibly believe in things like that, may also, almost in the same breath, admit that he admires and even envies such faith. So what is this thing called faith which arouses such negative responses and, at the same time, other, quite inconsistent reactions? In the Gospels Jesus is constantly praising faith, insisting that without it nothing is possible. Perhaps this book should have begun with faith. Instead, I end with it because one can't understand how a Christian can be a better person than a simply good person who has no belief, until one appreciates the role of faith in the moral life. This helps to explain why Jesus talks so much about it.

In the first chapter we saw how religious belief is not essentially different from all the other beliefs we hold with certainty, that if only logical and scientific proofs are acceptable, then we should have to abandon any claim that our dearest convictions are true. The same is true of religious faith, understood as the readiness to believe in what the Church believes. For trusting faith is by no means confined to religion; we use and depend on it every day of our lives. This is because we are not isolated individuals but interdependent members of the human community. If we demanded proofs in the sense just mentioned, it would be very hard even to get out of bed in the morning. Not that it would be easy to stay in bed either—for how do we know that the builder of our house didn't arrange for the roof to fall in on us after a period of time? How can we trust the train driver to get us to work in the morning? How can we even go out on the street at all when there may be somebody out there waiting to murder us?

On a deeper level, how can I make friends if I refuse to believe that anybody can like me, if I cannot bring myself to trust anyone else however friendly he may seem? It would be impossible ever to get married if one simply couldn't trust oneself to another person. Now, of course, it is true that sometimes our trust, our faith, in other people turns out to be misplaced. But the same applies even to "proofs." Our senses can deceive us. We were sure we saw a tree but it turned out to be a shadow; we were sure we added those figures up right but somehow we made a mistake. Yes, the possibility of making a mistake can never be ruled out. But equally, always to be allowing for the possibility, never being quite sure about anything, is what's called being oversuspicious, untrusting. We criticize people like that; we pity them for their inability to forge relationships. We don't admire skepticism of that sort.

And yet there are many people who think that skepticism, when it comes to religion, is not only necessary but commendable. Why should this be so in this area alone? Naturally, we shouldn't form our beliefs in religion or any other matter without good reasons, although as we've seen, to demand proofs of a certain kind, in matters where such proofs are wholly inappropriate, is both silly and wrong. When we do believe something with good reason, we should show a due measure of trust or faith. Othello should have been ready to trust Desdemona whatever the ostensible evidence Iago could bring. We blame Othello. We should also blame someone who has excellent reasons for believing that Christianity makes the best sense of the world that he can find, and yet refuses to trust the Word of God in the Bible, or somebody who becomes convinced that there is something about the Catholic Church that is compelling but draws back from trusting what the Church says. Just as in daily life, without that faith nothing can happen. That's why Jesus emphasizes faith.

The presence or absence of this faith has a significant effect on the moral life. Faith enables fallen human beings to be self-sacrificial, when otherwise it would be very hard for them to muster the necessary motivation to act in a way so apparently contrary to their interests. It gives a person the heart to practice the virtues; lacking it, as Jesus points out in a famous saying, the flesh is weak and unable to do much (see Mk. 14:38). For the Catholic Christian, faith is vital if the sacraments, which are not magic, are to take effect, and particularly if they are to enable the Catholic to "live on" Christ, thereby becoming Christlike. One can't live on bread and water if one's a celiac, nor can one live on lobster and champagne if one's allergic to shellfish. Analogously, one can't live on Christ in the Eucharist if one doesn't believe that what, to all appearances, are bread and wine are mysteriously and really the Body and Blood of Christ. The diet then doesn't change the person on it, any more than a diet high in nuts will give one the desired protein if nuts don't agree with one. A good or bad diet reveals itself in the person's physical health; that is also the idea of the spiritual diet that consists of Christ Himself.

Furthermore, faith makes possible the third great Christian virtue of hope. Like faith, hope may seem a pretty improbable sort of thing. What is it anyway? Hope looks forward to something one doesn't yet have, something perhaps one can't even imagine. Its importance is well recognized outside the religious sphere. A sick person is more likely to get better if he doesn't give up hope; a prisoner depends on hope simply perhaps to survive. Nobody sneers, however apparently desperate the situation, at anyone hoping against hope; far from it, we admire such a person. And the more hopeless things are, the greater is our admiration. If eventually the seriously ill patient or the hostage lives to tell their story, they will testify how it was hope that kept them going. Far from pitying their sanguinity, we applaud their courage in going on hoping. The faith-filled Christian who, despite everything, goes on confidently looking forward to the fullness of happiness which he or she believes only God can ultimately bestow in heaven, is no more to be despised for his or her "groundless, idle" optimism, if only because it is this hope which, like his faith, empowers him to behave in ways that people without his hope can hardly imitate, lacking this dynamic resource.

One thing that faith and hope naturally lead to is prayer. And here one has to note a (perhaps) surprising phenomenon. The evidence from surveys shows that a very large number of people, who have no very definite religious beliefs, still regularly pray. Why do they pray and to whom do they think they are praying? It must seem a bit like throwing a bottle with a message inside into the sea, not knowing whether anyone will ever read it. Even if one does have a clear idea that one is speaking to God, God must seem remote. But if one believes that God, in the person of the Holy Spirit, makes His home in one, then one is in a very different, privileged position. God is no longer "out there" somewhere or other but right within one. Communication becomes a lot easier. But, again, there's a catch. If you don't believe you're a dwelling for the Spirit, you're not going to have this advantage. Prayer will be much more difficult, if only because you're having to do all the work; whereas, if the Spirit's inside you, He can surely be expected to help you. Then, as in the rest of the Christian life, one does one's bit, but God also helps out.

I was saying that faith is basic to life at every level because we're not islands on our own. We need other people because they take us out of ourselves, and being shut up inside oneself is not the happiest of things. Well, religious faith does the same thing. It takes one out of oneself and introduces one into the company of God, which is ultimately more liberating than the company of any other human being. Prayer is this faith in active touch with God, wrapped in conversation with God, or in contemplation of the Beloved. To escape from one's egoistic self is not only to find happiness, it is also to fall into that goodness which so evades our silly, self-absorbed selves. Surveys show that people with religious faith are happier than those without it; they also say that those who pray are happier than those who don't. And it's much easier to be good, and particularly loving to others, if one's happy in oneself.

I began this last chapter by saying that Catholics should be—even if in fact they are not always—better than other people. I went on to point out that the world seems to expect more of them, at least at their best. It is certainly often said that the Catholic Church demands more of its members than do other Christian churches. Maybe it does. But then it also offers more and provides greater resources.

Catholic for a Reason

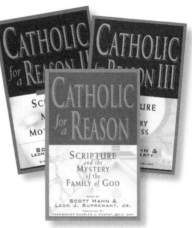

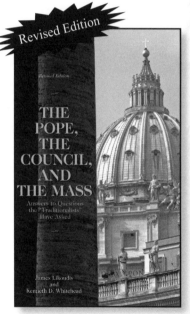

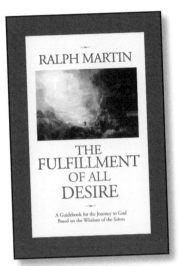

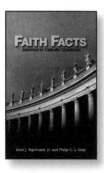
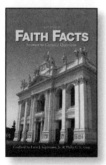

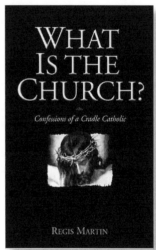